GI

("Guvmint" Issue)

Diane,

To fellow villager and neighbor. Hope you find some of these stories amusing, it was fun living them!

Best wishes & Enjoy the Book!

George McMurray
(g Lamar)

GI

("Guvmint" Issue)

The U.S. Army as Seen by GOBS (Good Ol' Boy Soldier) J. Lamar

LTC (RET)
George M. Massey

HILLSBORO PRESS
Franklin, Tennessee

Copyright 1997 by George M. Massey

All rights reserved. Written permission must be secured from the publisher to use or reproduce any part of this book, except for brief quotations in critical reviews and articles.

Printed in the United States of America

01   00   99   98   97   5   4   3   2   1

Library of Congress Catalog Card Number: 97–72017

ISBN: 1–57736–043–5

Illustrations by R. Daniel Proctor

Cover by Bozeman Design

Cover photo by Jacob Edwards

HILLSBORO PRESS
238 Seaboard Lane • Franklin, Tennessee 37067
800-321-5692

To two of the institutions which make ours the greatest nation on earth—family and the military. My family of Faye, Ellen, Suzanne and George—I love you. The military of fellow G.I.s—past, present, and future—I salute you.

Contents

Introduction ix
  Turning a Plowboy into a Marcher 1
  The How-to-Report-to-an-Officer Lesson 3
  How Not to Stand at Attention 4
  What You Can See Down the Muzzle of an M-1 Rifle 6
  What You Can Get from the M-1 Rifle: The M-1 Thumb 7
  Failing to Coordinate or Scaring the Hell Out of a Hospital 9
  ROTC Advanced Camp or Passage of Rites 11
  How Do You Decorate WWII Barracks? 12
  Wake Me Up When It's Over 13
  First Live PT (Physical Training) Formation or How Not to Impress Battalion Headquarters 15
  How Not to Show Up at Airborne PT Formation or The Black Hats Are Always Right 16
  The Holey T-Shirt or That's What Happens When You Get Dressed in the Dark 19
  How Not to Orient a Map with a Compass (on the Hood of a Jeep) 21
  Having 100% Participation Ain't Always Right 22
  The Juniors Skin the Seniors 24
  How to Wake Up a Stoned Housing (Drunk Soldier) 25
  Making an Arms Room Safer or Will a Steel Door Really Help? 28
  How to Count C-Rations 31
  Who Took What into Where? 33
  You Inspect What, When? 36
  How to Get to Umleitung or How Lost Am I? 38
  How to Make a Grown Man Cry 40
  Being on Guard Mount Can Be Scary 41

What Happened to the Rock?   44
The Five-Man Infantry Squad   46
Where Did You Say the Machete Is?   50
Play War Ain't the Real Thing   52
You Are Where? Doing What?   55
The Air Force Does It Again, But Wrong   58
Don't Break the Cookies   61
The Dangers of Cross-Country Skiing   62
Overrun by Viet Cong Ducks!   64
Did You Get the Luncheon Meat?   66
The Great Barge Chase or How Do You Lose a Boat That Big?   67
Reel in the Chicken   70
What Not to Do If You Have Hemorrhoids   71
There Will Be No Counting   73
God Is Alive and Well   74
A Defense Counselor's Nightmare   77
What Daylight Savings Time Does to a Schedule   79
Scout Dogs Are Not Trained to Attack (or So J. Lamar Thought)   81
Train the Dogs to Do What?   83
None the Wiser or What's in a Name?   86
It Takes How Many BUFEs to Load a Plane?   87
But They Won't Grow—Maybe It's the Dirt   89
Tricking the Major or How to Build Esprit de Corps   91
The Big Put Down   95
The CP (Command Post) Is Located Where?   98
You Swap the Old for the New or Was It New for the Old?   100
You Americans Never Learn   102
I Have One Hundred Tanks or Ich Habe ein Hundred Panzers   105
Where Are All the Spies?   107
Selling Hamburgers in Germany   109
I Beg Your Pardon   110
Dumpster 1, J. Lamar 0   112

Epilogue   115
Acronyms   116

Introduction

The army always has used, and will probably continue to use, acronyms (thought this was a type of sex perversion first time I heard it). As the title of this treatise shows, one of the most commonly known acronyms is that of GI—"Guvmint" Issue as a GOBS (Good Ol' Boy Soldier) would say it. Unless a person has been living under a rock out in the desert or wandering around in a moonshine-induced fog, he will have a fair-to-middling idea of what GI means. But will he know some of the more fun things GIs get into? Probably not. Enter GOBS, J. Lamar.

Now, J. Lamar ain't the sharpest bear from the woods. He did, however, get around a lot once he went through the metamorphosis (that's a high-toned way of saying "changed") from a slow-walking, slow-talking, tobacco-chewing plowboy to a slow-walking, slow-talking, tobacco-chewing soldier. So lay back or hunker down, depending on which position is your fancy, and look at the army as seen through the eyes of GOBS, J. Lamar.

All these vignettes (the French have a funny way of saying "short sketch") are based on real live happenings and some names may be similar. But, in order to keep from having obscene phone calls, voodoo curses, and possible bodily harm inflicted, the author has decided not to use real names (he may be dumb but he ain't stupid). In any event, it will also keep wives, children, family, and friends from knowing what some of their husbands, daddies, sons, and buddies really did in the war.

Turning a Plowboy into a Marcher

Had the Big Guy in the sky really wanted marching to be easy, most people (in particular, farm boys) would not have been born with a left foot. Because for some strange reason (might be that Prussian's influence from Revolutionary War days), the U.S. Army leads off in marching with the left foot. Of course, you have to lead with something and the left foot is it.

Enter J. Lamar and his friend from East Tennessee, Gerald Dean. These two met, literally on the drill fields of the University of

Tennessee, Knoxville, in the late 1950s. Everyone remembers this as the time of Elvis, blue suede shoes, rock-n-roll, duck-tail haircuts, and mandatory ROTC (Reserve Officer Training Corps) classes. If you thought J. Lamar was from the hills, he couldn't hold a full-blown torch to Gerald Dean. Why, Gerald Dean had no idea what dismounted drill (marching) was. He thought it might be a type of machine to plant corn, cotton, clover, and such.

J. Lamar knew something was amiss during drill when he kept feeling the heels of his shoes being hit while marching. Also, he had felt the wind from, and observed at close range, the sights of an M-1 rifle swing under his nose when the command "Rear, march!" was given. (Not sure how the army came up with this command, but I reckon it's better than "Turn around, march!" or "Go the other way, march!") The problem facing J. Lamar was that Gerald Dean could not stay in step and continually stepped on his heels and turned the wrong way on the command "Rear, march!"

Finally, J. Lamar's plight came under the gaze of Sergeant First Class Dinwiddie (no first name—"just Sergeant to you, *Kaydet!*"), who was keen of wit (somewhat), sharp of eye (though bloodshot most of the time), big of neck, and pointed of head. A throw-back to the old brown shoe army, so they say. Sergeant Dinwiddie's voice sounded like a load of pea gravel rolling off a tin roof. He apparently learned how to whisper in a saw mill. In addition, he did not carry on intimate conversations with "kaydets" as he verbally rendered them into a substance similar to silly putty, slime, and pond scum.

He swore at and to Gerald Dean that he would make him drill right, "If'n it were the last thing I do afore I go to coon hunter's heaven!" And, you know, he did.

Sergeant Dinwiddie used a simple technique. He gave Gerald Dean a rock to keep in his left hand and told him every time he heard "one," "hut," "three," or "left" while marching, his left foot had better be the lead foot and on the ground, or he would take Gerald Dean to the woods and run saw briars through his crotch. Now, for a country boy, this "treat" would not be looked upon as a fun thing to do. Surprisingly, and to the relief of J. Lamar, Gerald Dean's marching improved immediately.

However, Gerald Dean did have a hard time explaining to friends and neighbors why he always had a rock in his left hand. Could it be he was really a slow learner or did he think Sergeant Dinwiddie's threat about the saw briars carried over into "civilian walking"? One could only speculate.

The How-to-Report-to-an-Officer Lesson

As time progressed, J. Lamar eventually got on the personnel officer's list (not sure it was *that* list or not) to report. As previously indicated, J. Lamar was not totally attuned to the ways of the world, much less to the army's acronyms (there's that word again). J. Lamar was placed in a real quandary (he didn't know it was a quandary—he just knew he didn't know what to do) when he received a message in ROTC class which stated he should "Report to Major McNamara, ASAP."

Now, J. Lamar had been called a lot of names in his life but never ASAP. He didn't know what he had to do to be one. Well, after two days of cogitating (another one of those "ate" words J. Lamar did without the slightest idea of what it meant), he finally sauntered (that's similar to the way a big Holstein milk cow that hasn't been milked in two days makes her way to the stall—real slow and easy) into the major's office. When J. Lamar got to the major's desk, he did the unpardonable sin. He leaned over and placed his hands on the brightly shining, freshly polished surface.

Now, Major Mac (those who either knew him or did not value their life called him Major Mac) had not looked up at the sauntering J. Lamar. All J. Lamar had seen was the top of the major's bald head. As they say, some heads are made perfect; the others are covered with hair. Major Mac's should have been covered. His head not only had "knowledge knots" and rolls of fat but also had assorted warts, hairy moles, and scars (it was rumored he had a propensity for getting drunk and running headfirst into walls).

When the major detected the presence of J. Lamar (the grimy hands on the shiny surface of his desk), he slowly raised his head and confronted J. Lamar with a look that was a cross between a very mad ape and a traffic cop from the lower Bronx (I understand the New York types will know what I mean). With a loud, rapid fire "GETYOURHANDSOFFMYDESKGETOUTOFMYOFFICEWHOTHEHELLAREYOUCOMEBACKWHENYOULEARNHOWTOREPORT" blast, the major blew J. Lamar into the hallway. Feeling like someone had caught his head between two cymbals just after an eighteen-wheeler had run over him, J. Lamar stumbled (no longer in the sauntering mode) into Staff Sergeant Conway.

Compared to rough and uncouth Sergeant Dinwiddie, Sergeant Conway was urbane (what country folks would call being smooth around the edges). He calmed J. Lamar down, asked him what had happened (turned away to laugh when he found out), explained ASAP means "as soon as possible," and gave J. Lamar a thorough ten-minute class on reporting to an officer. After a few practice runs, Sergeant Conway directed J. Lamar to the major's office. Standing outside with his fingers crossed and his eyes looking heavenwardly, he hoped J. Lamar would perform well (or as they say back home, hoped he "done good").

J. Lamar didn't let him down.

He knocked loudly, marched in smartly, rendered a sharp hand salute, and sounded off like he had a set (you know what I mean). The major, being short of memory and duly impressed by J. Lamar, gave him a "warm fuzzy" (a more endearing term for an "attaboy") when he left.

At this point in his budding military career, J. Lamar began to understand why the army kept NCOs (noncommissioned officers) around. They literally and figuratively saved lives.

How Not to Stand at Attention

One of the fun things "kaydets" had to participate in each week involved dismounted drill (remember Gerald Dean?) with the

M-1 rifle (more on this piece of weaponry later). Also involved in drill is the position of attention. For the uninitiated, this position has some very intricate and precise factors—head up, chin down, shoulders back, stomach in, buttocks tucked, fingers curled with the thumb and forefinger touching and placed along the seam of the trousers (not britches, you hillbilly), heels together with the feet placed at a forty-five-degree angle. In other words, a rather uncomfortable way to stand out in the hot sun or in the wind on a cold day.

Don't even think about scratching that itchy place or wiping that runny nose. One of these attention-breaking movements would bring screaming people from every direction. Even moving the eyes to watch a wasp try to enter the ear of the "kaydet" next to you was not allowed. Breaking attention was considered worse than breaking wind, which some wiseacre would invariably do at the worse time—while the inspecting officer was in front of you.

Anyway, J. Lamar had perfected this position fairly well—so he thought.

During drill on a hot spring day, the entire "kaydet" corps (another French word which means a "bunch") had been placed in the position of attention. J. Lamar gave it his best but with one small problem—he had locked his knees. If you are keen of wit and sharp of mind, you remember locking of the knees was not part of the position of attention.

For those of you who have been there, you know what happened next. In very short order, blood flow in his lower extremities (ain't nothing vulgar—just his legs) became constricted. Before J. Lamar knew what hit him, his eyes crossed, his head felt as light as the fuzz on a flea's butt, he turned whiter than a KKK robe, and then pitched forward so the first point of contact with the ground was his nose. Looked something like a falling loblolly pine. Of course, no one else dared break attention. Finally, J. Lamar, looking like a linebacker who had forgotten to wear his helmet, was helped off the drill field by Sergeant Dinwiddie (remember him?). Sergeant Dinwiddie proceeded to lecture him in his inimitable style about how J. Lamar was "dumber than a stump fer lockin' yore knees at the position of attention." J. Lamar didn't have to be hit in the head with a two-by-four to remember this lesson!

What You Can See Down the Muzzle of an M-1 Rifle

For those of you who have been paying attention, the M-1 rifle has been mentioned previously and the author said more would be discussed about it later. This is later now.

The army used the M-1 rifle as its official rifle from 1936 to 1960 (thought you needed to know some trivia). One of the things done with the M-1, in addition to making holes in targets and assorted other things, was to conduct a maneuver known as "inspection, arms." As this maneuver implies, the M-1 required periodic inspections which in turn required periodic cleanings which in turn required "kaydets" to learn how to clean as well as present the weapon for inspection.

Now, for the uninitiated, cleanliness of weapons in the U.S. Army is next to godliness and even holds its own against motherhood and apple pie in importance. Therefore, cleaning of one's weapon became a weekly chore or duty depending on one's view.

J. Lamar and his buddies made a happening of these cleaning sessions. One "kaydet" in particular stood out—Casey Mack Bryant Moore (someone with three last names has to stand out). Casey Mack had a hard time perfecting the art of cleaning the M-1 and received numerous demerits for having a dirty weapon. These demerits were either worked off by extra duty in the supply room or they would affect the final grade received in ROTC.

Casey Mack did receive one small measure of revenge during a regular drill day inspection. The inspecting officer, a rather rotund (nice way of saying fat), sarcastic captain, had placed his thumb in the open bolt in order to reflect light up the barrel. By doing this, one can look down the muzzle (the end where the bullet comes out, you ninny) to check the cleanliness of the barrel and detect minute (ain't talking about part of an hour here) bits of dirt.

The captain apparently found some dirt in Casey Mack's barrel.

In a loud voice (loud for a high-pitched voice which resembled scratching a blackboard with a fingernail), the captain asked Casey Mack, "What do you see down the barrel of this M-1, Kaydet?"

To which Casey Mack replied, "Well, Sir, I see the end of your thumb." To which the rest of the "kaydets" stifled their laughter and glee at the obvious putdown.

The demerits Casey Mack received were well worth it.

What You Can Get from the M-1 Rifle: The M-1 Thumb

Now for those of you who were really paying attention, you remember we talked about "inspection, arms" with the M-1 and that it involves the use of the thumb. The thumb is used not only as a means to inspect the barrel but also to help close the bolt.

Not to get into a detailed dissertation (fancy way of saying "talking about something") of the intricacies of "inspection, arms," suffice it to say the right thumb is used to help close the bolt by depressing a spring which allows the bolt to go forward when released. The rub comes when the thumb is not removed quickly enough and the spring-loaded bolt slams it against the chamber end of the barrel (that's where the bullet goes in the barrel, you ninny). The bolt comes forward with the force and speed of a bunch of shoppers at a door buster sale! When the thumb gets caught between these two objects, it usually gets pulverized into a painful, bloody mess.

When bolts are closed in a mass formation, it can be a thrilling sound—like the shutting of a steel door—if all go forward at once. It can also sound like the typewriter pool of a large office if they are not in unison. Or, it can sound like what happened to one of J. Lamar's friends—Billy Joe Hightower.

During one such mass formation as mentioned above, the bolts closed with the resounding steel door sound but with one notable exception. Billy Joe was the unfortunate soul who did not remove his thumb quickly enough. As the bolts crashed forward in unison, a loud "Aw shit!" emanating from Billy Joe's throat resounded across the drill field, much to the consternation and chagrin of the ROTC cadre (another French word meaning "the bunch in charge").

This consternation did nothing to help the bloody M-1 thumb of Billy Joe Hightower.

Failing to Coordinate or
Scaring the Hell Out of a Hospital

Besides all the marching, cleaning of weapons, shining of shoes, close haircuts, and spiffy uniforms, ROTC training also included military tactics—how to fight and win wars. Of course, at the "kaydet" level, nothing, such as the invasion of Europe on D-Day, was required to teach tactics. Just a few simple sandbox exercises and locally run patrols would suffice.

The OIC (officer in charge) of the tactical training was a young, bright, energetic captain Elroy P. Walden. Captain Walden kept a straight sandbox and planned everything to the nth degree or as they say back home, "down to the gnat's ass." He came up with a bright idea which, on a scale of relativity, would have rivaled the invasion of Europe.

Those of you not familiar with the University of Tennessee and its location will be given a short lesson in geography. The campus is bounded on the east and south by the Tennessee River. The major portion of the campus during J. Lamar's time was located on a high piece of terrain oddly enough simply called "The Hill."

One could quickly discern the upper-class female students from the incoming women by a casual glance at their legs, in particular, their calves. Now for such a red-blooded male college student as J. Lamar, no one had to force a casual glance at legs—it was a full-time preoccupation. In any event, the number of uphill climbs and stair steps needed to reach the top of "The Hill," and more particularly the upper floors of Ayers Hall located on the top, developed calves. This was a precursor to the present-day step machines and came free of charge. So much for the geography lesson and anatomy development.

Back to tactical exercises. Captain Walden had developed a working relationship with the local marine reserve unit which had, among its many pieces of equipment, an old and very used amphibious truck known as a "duck." As the name implies, this truck could be used on land as well as in the water. In order to spice up the mundane tactical patrols used to teach the "kaydets" the finer points of small unit operations, Captain Walden's bright idea included the "duck" and the Tennessee River.

The overall plan called for the operation to proceed from the campus on the "duck," cross the river, make a landing on the bank, move through a wooded area by foot to attack an "enemy" base camp, and return to campus in the same manner. Of course, all this was to occur at night. Seemed simple enough. J. Lamar and his fellow "kaydets" thought this would be great fun and surely different. They didn't really worry about capsizing or hitting channel buoys, barges, or floating logs.

All went well for the operation up to and including the attack, which resulted in a clear victory over the infidel dogs of the enemy forces invading our homeland. The route to the base camp was relatively easy. Due to the fact that it was located up a small valley leading away from the river and that the "enemy" had a large bonfire blazing, getting misoriented was basically impossible.

The attack was carried out with all the loud noises of artillery simulators, firing of blank rounds, and psychologically uplifting screams and shouts of the attacking "kaydets." The enemy forces were all killed or captured and the withdrawal to the river to catch the "duck" back to campus began.

However, one major glitch became evident.

Heretofore undisclosed is the fact that the University of Tennessee Medical Center and Hospital Complex was located on the high ground across the Tennessee River from the main campus. More particularly, the complex was located above the enemy base camp so that the attack noise created much consternation among the staff and patients. Seems as if the young captain had failed to coordinate with anyone to inform them what would be happening.

The police and sheriff's offices were alerted. The air soon became alive with sirens and flashing lights which contributed even more to the palpitations of the petrified patients. At this point, it became a blinding flash to the captain what had happened.

J. Lamar and his fellow patrol members just hoped they wouldn't be arrested for disturbing the peace since for once they were only doing what they had been instructed to do. The marine gunnery sergeant driving the "duck" quickly figured out the situation and

George M. Massey

lamented on the possibilities of his being court-martialed. The captain, if the truth be known, probably came close to rendering his underwear unserviceable.

Order finally prevailed and the contingent under the captain's control made its way back across the river to the campus. The "kaydets" never really found out how much trouble the captain was in. They only knew he gave wide berth to the colonel in charge of the ROTC Department and certainly emphasized the need to properly coordinate when planning any type of operation. In reality, the "kaydets" learned more than tactics from the amphibious raid at the expense of one of the cadre. It was, however, one of the only times they gained experience from a foul-up other than their own.

ROTC Advanced Camp or Passage of Rites

Once the cadre had molded the "kaydets" for three years, the next big event in the ROTC metamorphosis (those who were paying attention in the introduction remember that word) occurs between the junior and senior years of ROTC—Advanced Camp. This is the six weeks of fun, frivolity, frenzy, but mostly futility in getting the "kaydets" to learn the finer points of becoming a commissioned officer. Leadership positions are rotated among the campers—all getting their chance in the barrel. Some do great, some do okay, some just do, and others fall flat on their faces. But as the saying goes, "Good judgment comes from experience; experience comes from bad judgement." Advanced Camp is one big "experience-gaining" exercise.

One of the major events each day was to get the "kaydets" loaded on to trucks known as "cattle cars." As the name implies, bodies are pressed together in the truck like cattle being taken to a stockyard to be sold. The cadre never did know how the instructions for loading these trucks evolved, but it became a daily routine that went something like this.

The "kaydet" company commander for the day would start issuing his commands for loading the trucks in a loud staccato burst of, "When

I say to fall out and fall in the trucks, I want the first platoon to fall out and fall in the first truck, the second platoon to fall out and fall in the second truck, the third platoon to fall out and fall in the third truck...." You get the picture. Just think, these young "kaydets" would get their start at Advanced Camp and might end up someday issuing orders which would move whole divisions and take less time to deliver.

The cadre tolerated this daily ritual because they didn't want to stifle initiative or curtail enthusiasm. However, one of J. Lamar's platoon mates really took initiative one rainy morning.

Instead of the normal rendition, this "kaydet," Joe Luther Scoggins, (yes, he went by both first names) came out with the command, "Y'all (yes, he was from the South) know what to do to load the trucks, so when I say 'DO IT!' do it!" And Joe Luther proceeded to command "DO IT!" With ponchos (raincoats to you civilians) dragging, "kaydets" laughing, and cadre grinding their teeth, the cattle cars were loaded in record time. Joe Luther received not only an "A" for trying, but an "ass-chewing" for an improper command. Didn't seem fair 'cause he got the trucks loaded. Just an example of some of the "experience" mentioned earlier.

How Do You Decorate WWII Barracks?

One of the finer points at Advanced Camp is the accommodations provided for the "kaydets." During World War II (the Big One), barracks were built by the thousands to last a few years or until the war ended. A great number of these buildings are still in use forty-five years later. Yes, the war did end, but the buildings remained.

The troop barracks were wooden-frame buildings, two stories high, a big open room on each floor with little to no decoration or interior amenities.

J. Lamar's platoon at Advanced Camp had one member who majored in interior decorating. This fact come out during a meeting with the company TAC officer—a Captain Forberg who apparently had not smiled anytime in the recent past and for sure not while at

Advanced Camp. His demeanor was the cross between an old maid librarian and an old skinflint banker. Nice guy!

The meeting concerned the overall condition of the barracks and what could be done to make them look better. Of course, Captain Forberg was implying cleanliness and general orderliness of the barracks.

Not so for one enterprising "kaydet." He put forth the idea that maybe rugs and curtains could help the appearance. The look he received from Captain Forberg would have penetrated five inches of homogeneous steel. But before Captain Forberg could render a verbal blast at such a ridiculous suggestion, the interior decorating major, "Kaydet" John Willie Ross Monroe (yes, he used all three front names) made a correction to the suggestions.

"Kaydet" Monroe stated, "Oh, no! Not rugs and curtains but carpets and draperies." This comment caused the platoon to break up in gales of laughter to which Captain Forberg even broke into a big, huge Mona Lisa smile.

It was one of those moments which created esprit and camaraderie within the platoon. However, the carpets and draperies did not materialize during Advanced Camp. They became the subject of numerous considerations as to color schemes, texture of cloth—anything to get the "kaydets'" minds off the daily grind.

Wake Me Up When It's Over

The last major event of Advanced Camp is the FTX (Field Training Exercises) where all previous training is put to the test. It tested how well the instruction had been presented, how well it had been received, but most of all, it tested who would break first—the cadre or the "kaydets."

J. Lamar's platoon had been placed in a defensive position in order to stop the advancing "hordes." They moved into position late in the afternoon after having marched with full field packs and weapons through the hot, humid Fort Benning terrain. Not that they were already hot and sweaty enough but upon reaching the defensive position, the platoon was given the order to dig in—not C-rations (combat rations) or mess hall chow, but to dig in as in foxholes. So, with darkness quickly approaching, the "kaydet" chain of command was just about at its breaking point.

Mingled with the sounds of entrenching tools (those little shovels used for a variety of different jobs) were comments of "kaydets" who were less than happy with their present status in life.

Just as the foxholes were completed, the weather gods came alive with a drenching downpour which, coupled with the already miserable feeling, made the night one to remember. There isn't a worse feeling than to be soaking wet from sweat and have to cover up with a poncho that immediately becomes a clammy, slick piece of impervious rubberized material clinging all over like a wet T-shirt on a big-busted sorority girl at the beach.

Once the rain stopped and after the foxholes had conveniently filled up with water, the fog rolled in and the night turned cold. The clammy poncho now became too uncomfortable to wear but the coolness of the night went through to the bone if you took it off. Add to this mosquitoes which could stand flat-footed and rape turkeys and it became a night of total discomfort—unlike any J. Lamar had ever experienced. As the night wore on, his skin began to wrinkle, shrivel, and itch. That's right, itch. Staying awake was no problem.

Just as it became almost too much to bear, the first rays of day broke over the position. As the sun rose higher, the fog lifted, the mosquitoes left, and J. Lamar's clothes started to dry out, it became almost bearable. The attacking "hordes" had not come at night, so the platoon began bracing for the battle to come. That is, all but one "kaydet" in the next foxhole who could have been heard in the next county: "Wake me up when it's over."

However, unbeknownst to J. Lamar and his foxhole buddy, one of the cadre—a Lieutenant Colonel Mitch—whom the "kaydets" had given a rhyming three word nickname, had walked up behind their position. There he stood in a pith helmet, short khaki pants, gray knee socks with his hands on his hips. That's right, the army used to have a summer uniform such as described above. He looked like a WWII British officer somewhere in the South Pacific.

LTC Mitch stepped up to the foxhole next to J. Lamar's and in a loud voice stated, "I'm waking your ass up and I ain't even started!" The "kaydet" was then led into the pine thicket behind the position for a short but apparently hard counseling session about attitude, when to sleep, etc. The platoon did, by the way, repel the attacking "hordes."

First Live PT (Physical Training) Formation or How Not to Impress Battalion Headquarters

J. Lamar's progress through the ROTC program culminated with his receipt of the coveted gold bar of a second lieutenant (otherwise known as a butter bar). Then, in 1962, he went to his first assignment and first unit—a rifle company at Fort Benning, Georgia, "Home of the Infantry, Queen of Battle." Now, artillery types say that artillery is the "King of Battle" and always puts its shots where the Queen wants it—there is debate on this.

Back to J. Lamar's first assignment.

The rifle company J. Lamar joined had an XO (executive officer)—the person who knows all, does all, and scares all second lieutenants. This XO was the cross between a bantam rooster and a mean grizzly bear—had the rooster's size and the bear's disposition. You know the type.

The first meeting between the XO and J. Lamar resulted in J. Lamar receiving his first major mission. It was *not* did he want to, did he know how to, but that he would conduct PT (physical training) formation for the company the next morning. Now this meant being out in front of some 150 soldiers leading them through the army's daily dozen (ain't a bunch of donuts or body functions we're talking about). The daily dozen is a series of exercises designed to make the body sore if one is not in condition.

J. Lamar had "done good," as they say, up through the daily dozen. He then took the company on a run through the streets of the post. Along this route, they passed the battalion headquarters. Now J. Lamar had been counting cadence and leading the company in certain risque (French way of saying "off-color") chants. The one that caught the attention of the battalion staff, however, was not off-color but rather degrading. As J. Lamar led the company by the headquarters, all heads held high, shoulders back and leather lungs shouting, he started the chant,"on the left, sick call!"

Needless to say, there was a reception committee, led by the XO, waiting back at the company. J. Lamar just barely escaped sick call himself. After dismissing the company, who had taken an immediate liking to this young, energetic, but dumb lieutenant, J. Lamar reported to the XO who proceeded to chew him out like a pit bull chewing on a toy poodle. Less than a week in his first assignment, J. Lamar had received his first assignment and "ass-chewing" on the same day. Not bad for a butter bar (the affectionate name given to second lieutenants by troops, NCOs, and little old ladies in tennis shoes). However, as the saying goes, "what goes around, comes around" or "he who laughs last, laughs best." J. Lamar did witness the XO lose a portion of his posterior. More on this later. On to other PT trials and tribulations.

How Not to Show Up at Airborne PT Formation or The Black Hats Are Always Right

One of the fun things they do in the military is jump or parachute from perfectly good airplanes. Some people view this activity as rather dumb, but, at least, the only sudden stop is with the ground and not a bunch of wild drivers on the streets and highways of America. Your chances for injury are much higher on the streets and highways.

In any event, J. Lamar volunteered to attend Airborne School at Fort Benning, Georgia. Successful completion of this school allowed J. Lamar to wear the coveted jump wings, a glider patch on his overseas cap (this piece of headgear has a more endearing name due to its style and shape—the uninitiated will remain uninitiated), and spit-shined boots. Of course, his mother thought she had raised an idiot when she found out he had jumped from a perfectly good plane.

One of the activities involved with airborne training is PT. Yes, the physical training we discussed before. The major difference is the PT formations are conducted by NCOs who the army had to search long and hard to find. They are called the "black hats" and, as the name implies, they are the bad guys. All have leather lungs, no body fat, piercing eyes, and can ask more questions with seemingly no correct answers.

There is a reason for this. One of the favorite exercises of the "black hats" is the push-up or as they called it "pushing away Georgia." The push-up helps strengthen the upper body as well as

developing what is known as the push-up muscle. This muscle, if a proper PLF (parachute landing fall) is executed, would be one of the five points of contact with the ground—balls of the feet, side of the calf or lower leg, side of the thigh, the buttocks, and the above mentioned push-up muscle or upper back area. Of course, most PLFs have three points of contact with the ground—heels, ass, and back of the head. Fortunately, all jumpers must wear helmets, which lessens this shock somewhat.

The push-up is used extensively as a motivator to do things correctly or a student would push away Georgia in a series of twenty repetitions each. These repetitions were given for incorrect answers to questions asked by the "black hats." Examples of some of these real astute questions are "How many belt loops are on your fatigues?"; "How many eyelets do your boots have?"; "How many buttons do your fatigues have?"; "What is my first name?" (you had better answer, Sergeant); and "How tall is the main post flagpole?" You get the idea.

Well, enter J. Lamar into this world of questioning and pushing away Georgia. As you might guess, he became very proficient at pushing away Georgia.

The one situation, however, that got him the most repetitions resulted from his haircut or lack thereof. At this time in the army, the haircut style worn most was the "white sidewall." J. Lamar thought he had one. But he received severe and direct counseling from the "black hats" during the first formation for having hair that looked like the cross between a shaggy sheep dog and a bull buffalo. Not to be outdone, J. Lamar went home that night and shaved round his head to a point three inches above his ears.

Now, this was not a pretty sight. The "black hats" had a field day the next morning. Between the snickers and snide remarks such as "Is that a cue ball with hair or what?"; "It looks smooth and pink as a baby's butt"; "The way the rest of his hair sticks out would make an orangutan feel proud," J. Lamar got to practice the push-up maneuver numerous times. After only two formations, he became a true believer that the "black hats" are always right.

The Holey T-Shirt or
That's What Happens When You Get Dressed in the Dark

The next major faux pas (no, it ain't pronounced fox pass and it is a French way of saying "fouling up") J. Lamar committed had to do with a T-shirt he wore one day to PT formation. Not only did haircuts have to be correct, boots shined, fatigues starched, belt buckles shined, and faces clean shaven, all other items of the uniform had to be clean and in good repair.

Well, J. Lamar got through the initial morning inspection with no problems and along with the other students retired to the sawdust pit for PT. Right away those of you who are keen of wit and sharp of mind are thinking wouldn't the sawdust pit screw up the spit-shined boots, starched fatigues, and overall cleanliness of the students? You got it!

An exercise known as arm circles is an excruciating maneuver for those with heavy arms. The arms are held out to the side at shoulder height with the fingers extended and joined together, palms up, and the arms are rotated in small circles.

After a few minutes of rotating your arms, it feels like a track team with spikes is running across the top of your shoulders. J. Lamar had reached this point of "ecstasy" when he had the eerie feeling that someone was looking at his left armpit.

He was correct.

A "black hat" with his piercing eyes had correctly perceived that J. Lamar had committed the unpardonable sin of wearing a T-shirt with a hole in it (that happens when you dress in the dark and don't check for holes).

Other "black hats" were called over to confirm if in fact that the shirt did have a hole in the armpit. One wondered, in loud tones, if possibly J. Lamar had caught his toe in the hole while putting it on. Another surmised that the hole was to let his hairy armpit breathe. All the while, J. Lamar had to continue the arm circles and wonder how many times the rest of the day he would have to push away Georgia for having a "holey T-shirt." At least it took his mind off the spikes in his shoulders and made him vow that in the future he'd check his uniform before going to bed. J. Lamar slowly learned how to stay a step ahead but only at the expense of his push-up muscles.

Of course, it would make the PLFs easier and softer—of course.

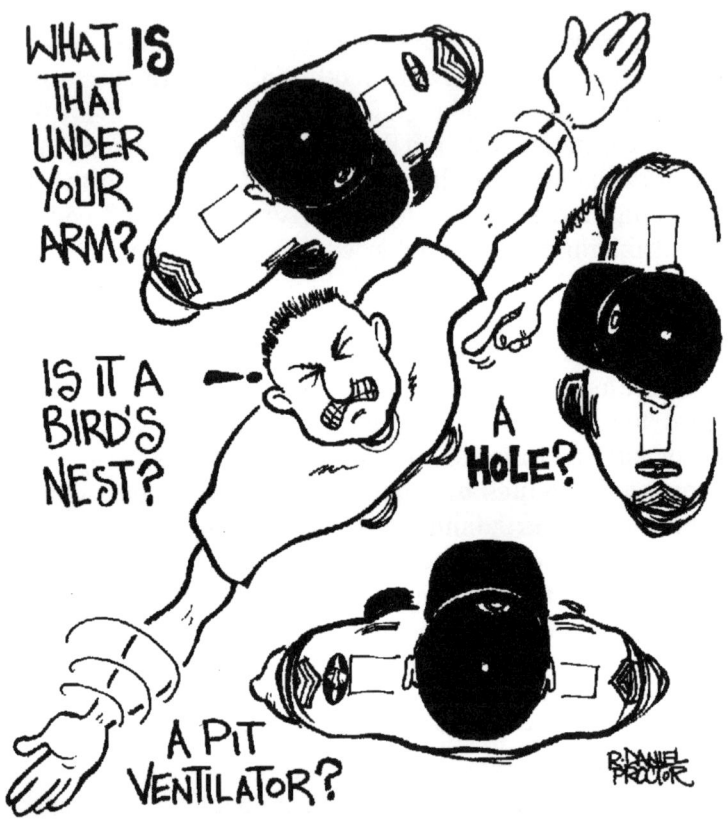

How Not to Orient a Map with a Compass (on the Hood of a Jeep)

Having survived the rigors of learning to jump from a perfectly good aircraft, J. Lamar returned to his infantry company to continue his military career.

A facet of the military is the FTX (field training exercise) or as some of the military wives called it—"big" Boy Scout camping trip. FTXs gave the staff and commanders an opportunity to try out plans and check the status of training of the soldiers or in many cases, the lack thereof. FTXs gave the soldiers the opportunity to get away from cleaning latrines (bathrooms to you National Guard types), shining floors, making up their bunks, and other housecleaning chores connected with living in the barracks.

FTXs also presented the opportunity for eating C-rations or in modern-day lingo—MREs or meals ready-to-eat. This does not mean C-rations are not ready-to-eat but points up how the Pentagon (the five-sided funny farm on the Potomac) changes nomenclature of items every few years to keep all on their toes.

However, the most important thing about FTXs is the opportunity they gave certain people to show off their ignorance. J. Lamar witnessed one such display.

J. Lamar had a fellow lieutenant, a big, red-faced know-it-all Texan, named Tyler Wayne Haldane (his momma and daddy had to have been closet poets to come up with that name). Now everyone but his southern belle type wife, Romana Louise, called him "Tex." She called him "Tiela Wain, Darlin'."

Anyway, Tex or "Tiela Wain" received a mission to lead the company cross-country. The first thing he began to do was to make a map recon to determine the route to take. Part of this process is to orient the map with the surrounding terrain (hills, creeks, ridgelines—all those things put there by nature). Another part is to determine the direction one desires to take. This can be done by matching the map direction with the compass direction. You place the compass on top of the map and orient the grid lines on the map with the direction of the north-seeking arrow of the compass.

Tex decided to use the compass method to get himself oriented so he could lead the company across hill and dale. One small problem. He placed the map on the hood of a jeep and began to orient the map using his compass which was also on the hood.

All standing around observing this did not fall over themselves to tell Tex the egregious (one of those pointy-headed professor ways of saying "bad") mistake he was committing. Even the most rear rank private knows the metal in the jeep would throw the compass off.

Apparently Tex was none the wiser until the company first sergeant, Sergeant Travis Leon Leatherwood (his last name should give a clue as to how hard he was) pointed out in graphic terms how the "Loutenant was about to get the whole galdarn company more lost than a sailor in a Saturday night Holy Roller meeting."

"Tiela Wain, Darlin'" had a hard time explaining this situation to the rest of the battalion lieutenants during the next happy hour at the Officers' Club.

Of course, this incident made its way back to the faculty at the infantry school as a real life example of how not to orient a map with a compass. Think maybe J. Lamar and some of his buddies had anything to do with this?

Having 100% Participation Ain't Always Right

Many times people are faced with situations where their head says do one thing but their heart says do another.

J. Lamar faced such a situation with reference to pay day contributions which were mandatory for the soldiers. These contributions were to organizations such as AER (Army Emergency Relief or as some wags called it "Ain't Ever Received"), American Red Cross, Old Soldiers Home, Soldiers and Sailors Widow Fund, First Sergeant's Fund (for his "fun," I guess), and any number of other worthwhile causes. It became so bad that one month alone there were eight different contributions at the end of the pay line. The contributions were usually a dollar, but on a private's pay of some seventy-five dollars a month, a dollar each was a big chunk.

J. Lamar felt enough was enough. He decided to make his stand the next month when the company commander, Captain Westcott Andrew Regent (with a name like that he was fortunate his initials spelled WAR), put out the edict (which means "I don't want to hear any bitching or moaning") that there would be one hundred percent participation for the aid to the Post Humane Society Fund. No set amount as to individual contribution was decreed. Now J. Lamar didn't have any axes to grind with lost and wayward animals but he wanted to make a point. He called his NCOs together and gave them his plan. The total number of soldiers in the platoon counting himself was forty-three. Therefore, J. Lamar struck upon the bright idea that 100 percent participation would be satisfied by turning in forty-three cents. This is what he did.

You guessed it. J. Lamar had an immediate meeting with Captain WAR. Westcott may be a funny sounding name, but the captain apparently had had to fight the name situation all his life. Therefore, his disposition on a good day was similar to that of a bull elephant that had inadvertently sniffed cactus spines up his trunk. He would not win the Mr. Congeniality award at Boys State.

In any event, J. Lamar found himself in front of the captain trying to explain the real meaning of his platoon's contribution. Of course, there would be no explanation which would be satisfactory. The once bright idea lost its sheen in the verbal blast rendered by Captain WAR. His bellows were discernible three blocks away which, of course, included J. Lamar's platoon bay.

He may have, figuratively, lost a large portion of his posterior, but J. Lamar did gain a large measure of respect from the platoon for trying the 100 percent participation approach. In later years, the monthly pay day contributions gave way to a once a year "your fair share is $_____" based on rank. This eventually gave way to a totally voluntary system of contributing. J. Lamar may have been a little ahead of the times with his approach, but he secretly felt he had started the ball rolling with his stand.

The Juniors Skin the Seniors

Soon after arriving at Fort Benning, their first duty station, J. Lamar and his bride of four years, Peggy Sue Ann, came to realize there were many social functions to attend when the units were not in the field training. Of course, the wives got together while the men were away to swap recipes, shopping tips, ways to keep babies from crying, how to deal with the post engineers, and various other need-to-know items. This created a type of female bonding similar in nature to the bonding process occurring between their husbands and the soldiers. And, if you can believe it was similar, beware of real estate agents selling mountain property in Florida.

One of the first functions J. Lamar and Peggy Sue Ann attended was a casual penny, nickel, dime poker party hosted by a crusty major and his wife. The major, Bobby Paul Westall, was a throwback to the old brown shoe army (i.e., World War II and Korea) who truly felt any lieutenant should be seen and not heard. Actually, he thought lieutenants should stay in the field training or pulling duty so they wouldn't be seen as well. But Bobby Paul did like poker and he did like to entertain. J. Lamar and Peggy Sue Ann arrived, along with four other couples, all captains, to compete in poker. This made J. Lamar and Peggy Sue Ann younger in age and junior in rank.

J. Lamar had a fair knowledge of which poker hands should be bet on and which should be folded. Peggy Sue Ann only knew that some of the cards had valentines, some had shovel-like figures, some had squares turned sideways, and some had faces with only one eye, and that cards only came in two colors—black and red. This was going to be a fun evening. It might also be mentioned that as the junior couple in rank, J. Lamar and Peggy Sue Ann did not come to the party with a deep pocket of money. In those days, a lieutenant's pay went about as far as a cheap bottle of wine in a carload of winos.

The participants were divided into two tables of six. Bobby Paul had a standing rule—no husband and wife could be at the same table. This would appear to have left Peggy Sue Ann at a big disadvantage since she wouldn't have J. Lamar to give her a few quick lessons, kick her under the table, or glare at her. Not to worry,

Bobby Paul proceeded to give her a short lesson on the rudiments of poker and stated he wouldn't let her lose too heavily. In particular, the basic game played was five-card stud with nothing wild. Pretty well meant what you saw was what you got.

There is the old saying—a blind hog will find an acorn. Well, J. Lamar and Peggy Sue Ann stayed blind all night and found most of the acorns. It was one of those rare situations where the underdogs came out on top in a big way. Peggy Sue Ann quickly got the hang of what was meant by having three cards of the same face, even though some only had one eye, or having five of the same figure (valentines, shovels, dog tracks, or sideways squares), or having five cards in sequence, etc. She didn't know what to call the hands, but she knew the other participants were calling her hands a lot of names, not really referring to the cards. J. Lamar enjoyed the same run of luck at his table, and before the evening was over, he could have built a fortified bunker from the pile of pennies, nickels, and dimes on the table in front of him. Peggy Sue Ann very meticulously stacked her winnings in neat rows in front of her seat. As her rows grew longer, Bobby Paul became more agitated but, being a good host, did not let it show. He just consumed more and more Black Jack and branch (water to you Yankee types).

Pretty soon the bloodletting ended. J. Lamar and Peggy Sue Ann swept their winnings of pennies, nickels, and dimes into a brown paper bag and told Bobby Paul and the rest how much they had enjoyed the evening. Bobby Paul through a tight grin with gritted teeth said, "I'm sure you did and we're glad you came." Half a statement being true ain't all bad. Believe it or not, J. Lamar and Peggy Sue Ann were invited back to other poker outings. The "seniors" had to try to get their money back from the "juniors."

How to Wake Up a Stoned Housing (Drunk Soldier)

Platoon leaders, such as J. Lamar, were faced with various day-to-day situations which sometimes required direct and immediate action to make a point. Such was the case on the morning after his company had been in the field for a week. Upon returning to the barracks, equipment and personal gear had to be cleaned and maintained. The army calls it POM (Post Operation Maintenance).

Well, during one session of POM, J. Lamar's platoon sergeant, Sergeant First Class Jeremiah (Hoot) Gibson (seems like all Southern males with the last name Gibson are nicknamed Hoot) came into the platoon leaders' room and reported to J. Lamar that they could not get Private Alphonso Leroy Terry out of bed. Seems as though Private Terry had attempted to drink all the booze he could find east of the Mississippi River the previous evening.

J. Lamar was totally astounded that the platoon sergeant and squad leader were unable to get a private out of bed. Turning over his bunk would have been one way. At least, Alphonso Leroy would have been out of bed. Grabbing Alphonso Leroy and picking him up bodily would have been another. J. Lamar used another technique. One which he demonstrated in front of the entire platoon.

Private Terry was on his back, fully clothed, mouth open, snoring like a band saw cutting through hard oak wood. A perfect setup for the wake-up technique J. Lamar employed.

Filling a five-gallon trash can full of water, J. Lamar proceeded to stand over Alphonso Leroy's bed and shout into his ear in his loudest platoon leader's voice "Platoon, Attention!" Somewhere in the dark, drunken recesses of his brain, or stoned housing as it were, Alphonso Leroy must have heard the command because his eyelids popped open to reveal eyeballs dancing around like beads of water on a hot griddle.

Just at that moment, J. Lamar let fly with the full trash can of water direct at the open mouth and eyes. Amid the gales of laughter and catcalls from the rest of the platoon, Alphonso Leroy came off the bunk like a dog whose balls had been touched by a red hot poker. Before Alphonso Leroy could figure out what had happened, J. Lamar had grabbed and braced him against the wall and let him know in no uncertain terms that for the rest of the POM period, Private Terry had better be standing and maintaining equipment every time J. Lamar came into the platoon bay.

Alphonso Leroy, once his senses let him know he was wet and cold and that J. Lamar had been responsible, decided to go "whup

the platoon leader's ass." He made one small mistake. He made the declaration in front of Sgt. Larsel "Boom-Boom" Perry, a member of the division's boxing team.

Of course, Sergeant "Boom-Boom" decided that because Alphonso Leroy had left his appointed place of duty, he could intervene. Alphonso Leroy made his second mistake. He took a big roundhouse swing at Sergeant "Boom-Boom" who hit Alphonso Leroy flush on the nose like a red-headed, blacked-back, three-toed woodpecker hitting a tree full of piss ants—hard and continuous.

Needless to say, Alphonso Leroy never made it to J. Lamar. He, along with the rest of the platoon, now knew how to wake up a stoned housing (drunk soldier). The NCOs coined a new phrase used to get soldiers out of bed: "I'll use the lieutenant's wake-up call on you."

J. Lamar had fun at the next happy hour telling the other lieutenants the success he had with the trash can of water. Strangely enough, J. Lamar never had another opportunity to use the technique.

Making an Arms Room Safer or Will a Steel Door Really Help?

Speaking of direct actions to make a point, J. Lamar got the opportunity to witness the NCO Corps in operation in its finest tradition. Understand that all military units have various characters who spice up the day-to-day operations. His company was no exception. Two of the biggest characters were probably the most important members of the company—the supply sergeant and the mess sergeant. They were drinking buddies from the Korean War.

In particular, the supply sergeant, Staff Sergeant Winfred L. Ready, was known far and wide for his propensity to consume copious amounts of alcohol resulting in extended "supply runs" sometimes lasting three to four days. He always came back with a truckload of unaccounted-for equipment and supplies. His rationale being: "Well, sir, it makes good trading material so I can make up the company's shortages." Made sense to J. Lamar. In addition, SSG Ready also had the uncanny ability to BS his way through inspections so that the company supply operations always came out looking good. Maybe the inspectors were also drinking buddies. No one ever asked.

However, during an inspection of the company's arms room by a newly assigned security NCO from the post provost marshall's office, otherwise known as the military police, it appeared SSG Ready had met his match. Based on a real strict interpretation of the security regulations (SSG Ready said it was a "chicken shit" interpretation), the security NCO determined the arms room to be unsecure and failing to meet the regulations. The reason? The door leading into the arms room from an inside hallway was not steel even though it was a solid door and had all the required locks. As you guessed by now, the arms room fell under the purview of the supply functions of the company, hence SSG Ready's involvement.

The security NCO's interpretation was technically correct but practically not really necessary. SSG Ready graphically proved his point.

Unbeknownst to the security NCO, the company had just received approval from the post engineers to do some modification to the building which included removing some concrete block walls

to make larger rooms of smaller rooms. SSG Ready had been involved in this type of modification in the past and had developed a quick method to tear down the major portions of the wall. He simply took a fifteen-pound sledgehammer and flailed away at the wall. The concrete blocks broke open like watermelons falling off the back of an overloaded flatbed truck going to market.

When told the arms room was unsecure due to the lack of a steel door, SSG Ready cocked his head sideways, shifted the stub of a cigar he always had in his mouth from one side to the other and said, "You want to see unsecure? I'll show you unsecured. The walls to the arms room are the same as the walls in the rest of the building. Come with me and I'll show you how to get in the arms room without going through your friggin' steel door!"

At this point, the security NCO was not sure what he was about to witness but he knew it probably wouldn't be pretty. SSG Ready grabbed the sledgehammer from behind his desk and took the security NCO down the hall to the soon-to-be renovated rooms. J. Lamar could see what was coming and quickly ran to get an audience to watch the "wall busting" as well as get the reaction of the security NCO who, by this time, looked like he was being led to his execution by sledgehammer.

Upon entering the room, SSG Ready told the security NCO to stand back and he would demonstrate the method used to get into the arms room without going through the door. The security NCO began pleading with SSG Ready that he really didn't need the demonstration because he believed SSG Ready and he didn't want to be part of the "wall busting." SSG Ready paid no attention and began his flailing.

With his first hit, three or four of the concrete blocks disintegrated, the security NCO turned white, dropped his inspection clipboard, and beseeched J. Lamar to stop this crazy fool. J. Lamar, getting into the mood of the moment, stated there ain't no way he was going to intercede against a wild-eyed man with a fifteen-pound sledgehammer in his hand. The security NCO regained control of his clipboard, changed the results of the inspection to satisfactory, got J. Lamar to sign off on it, and left the building in an almost dead run.

By this time, SSG Ready was up against the remaining wall shouting, "I showed the SOB about his friggin' steel door!" The rest of the witnesses began dispersing to tell the rest of the company about the latest exploit of SSG Ready. J. Lamar couldn't wait to get to happy hour and tell his fellow lieutenants. And strangely enough, no other reports came down through the channels concerning the arms room security.

How to Count C-Rations

J Lamar, along with the rest of his battlegroup, participated in a six-month exchange of assignment with another battlegroup from Germany. This program, known as "Rotaplan," involved actually moving all the personnel from Fort Benning, Georgia, to a "lovely" post in Germany named Baumholder, in honor of the village located nearby. The village consisted of seventy-nine bars, a bahnhof (railroad station), a town hall, and not much else. The bars should be a clue as to the principal business conducted—soak the GI for his hard-earned pay.

The training area of Baumholder had one other unique feature—any direction you drove away from the area went downhill and you would break out into sunshine after a few miles. It always seemed cloudy, rainy, and cold in Baumholder. Maybe this contributed as well to the high density of bars. Not much to do and you sure didn't want to do it outside.

Anyway, another part of the "Rotaplan" program involved the exchange of equipment and supplies—in particular, C-Rations (rations, combat is the designated name). The army's answer to prepackaged culinary delights or, in some circles, belly bombs. (Rating special mention are the ham and lima bean mix or beans with wieners combination.)

One of J. Lamar's first tasks upon arrival in Baumholder was to count the number of C-ration meals located throughout the company to include in the supply room, mess hall (now known as the dining facility), and loaded on the twenty some odd tracked APCs (Armored Personnel Carriers) used to transport the infantry soldiers through the countryside.

The reason for this verification was to ensure the company had its combat load on hand in case the Warsaw Pact forces (located in East Germany) became incited to riot and roared across the border to do battle. A soldier has to eat when fighting.

Remember the XO (executive officer) who had chewed on J. Lamar for his lack of discretion in leading his company past the battalion headquarters during PT? This same XO had signed for the equipment and supplies from another XO who had long since departed with his battlegroup to Fort Benning. Included in the supplies were some eight thousand individual C-ration meals.

However, and this is where the plot thickens and J. Lamar got the last laugh, the XO had counted by case and multiplied by eighteen to come up with the number of meals he signed over from the departed XO. One small problem. The old issue of C-rations did have eighteen meals per case. The new issue had twelve meals per case.

It doesn't take a math major to figure out what had happened. The XO had been had to the tune of 1,400 meals which in round figures amounted to approximately four thousand dollars.

When J. Lamar first reported this fact to the XO, he received a verbal blast similar to an agitated bull elephant. But J. Lamar had come prepared. He had the supply sergeant with him who, although not real sharp of mind or keen of wit, did know how to count. Of course, the XO had to be shown the error of his ways. When he realized what had transpired, all he could say was "Oh, shit!"

At that point, J. Lamar could only show compassion and understanding on the outside but on the inside he laughed and did one-handed backflips at seeing the XO sweat over the missing C-ration meals.

In the end, the XO received help from the supply sergeant and mess sergeant, who, being old drinking buddies, were able to do a watch-my-fingers-they-never-leave-my-hand accounting for C-rations during the next few FTXs. The missing meals were made up and J. Lamar had to no longer be that afraid of the XO. He did, however, keep it as an "ace in the hole."

George M. Massey

Who Took What into Where?

Sometimes when units go to the field for training, the situation is more administrative which results in slightly better field living and eating accommodations. You must understand that the military is a large corporation like GM, IBM, or other fortune 500 companies. However, there is widespread relativity when it comes to perks. Let me cite a few examples.

The CEO of a large corporation is usually driven to and from work and meetings in a professionally chauffeured limousine with all the latest in telephonic communications, leather upholstery, window tinting and other comfort amenities. In a field training setting, the commander, or CEO, of a unit is hauled around in a vehicle (i.e., jeep) with the latest in military combat radios, canvas upholstery, plastic side curtains, and the stiffest suspension system available. This is nice because rough roads sure work on the hemorrhoids and herniated discs.

When it comes to sleeping accommodations, even the worker bees in a civilian corporation have it better. When civilians are sent on a trip to receive training, at least they are given accommodations at a Motel Six, Red Roof Inn, or similar establishment with TV, hot showers, beds with sheets, and flush toilets. The soldier is given a shelter half which is put with the shelter half of one of his buddies to make a pup tent; a thin piece of sponge which serves as a mattress; a sleeping bag too hot for the summer and too cold for the winter; an entrenching tool and C-ration toilet paper to serve the call of nature in case he is too far from the slit trench or two holer if on a firing range; and rubber rain suits or ponchos to keep dry in case of rain—which it usually does during field training. The soldier gets to carry all this in a beautifully designed, olive drab-colored rucksack. The officers and commanders do have it better. They get to sleep on military cots in tents large enough to stand in. Everything else, as to accommodations, is basically the same. Sometimes shower points, which consisted of pallet floors and multiple shower heads in a communal setting, would be set up for the units. Not your standard motel or hotel accommodations.

One of the major differences centers around the dining facilities. In garrison, or the barracks setting, the military dining facilities (mess halls) would be similar to those of a corporate headquarters. The worker bees and soldiers have a cafeteria-type facility for their meals. Of course, the soldiers living in the barracks usually eat three meals a day in the mess hall; worker bees only eat lunch (or dinner for you southerners) in their cafeterias.

Now the CEO/commander/officer types do have a corner of the mess hall away from, but in sight of, the soldiers. The tables, chairs, condiments, stainless steel tableware, and trays are the same as used by the soldiers. In some cases, there is a mess hall orderly dressed in the army's newest BDU (battle dress uniform) or fatigues who does basic bus duties. The food is the same as served to the troops and is paid for before consumption.

Compared to this is the corporate dining rooms for high-level management types. These rooms are separate and apart from the regular cafeterias. Included are such amenities as plush carpet, exquisite decor for the walls, soft background music and lighting, sterling silverware, bone china, crystal water goblets, soft plush chairs, linen tablecloths and napkins, and a menu selection fit for a five-star restaurant. The waiters are very obsequious (pointy-headed way of saying they cater to every whim). They are so good they take orders without writing them down. A chit is signed which ultimately gets paid by a payroll deduction which precluded one from having to carry dirty money in one's pocket.

Enough of these comparisons and on to a situation in which J. Lamar and his C-ration counting XO found themselves.

Mentioned before was the fact that in a field training situation on a firing range, there would be two-holer latrines available. In J. Lamar's and his XO's particular case, modernization had arrived in the form of a four holer with individual stalls. This latrine, however, still had the long, bathtub-looking urinal tilted toward one end so it would drain, and all the cigarette butts would end up in one big clogging pile. Cleaning out urine-soggy cigarette butts was not one of the latrine orderlies biggest thrills. "How did one get tabbed for latrine orderly?" you ask. Piss off the company first sergeant.

In a firing range setting, the mess line was usually set up under tents so the cooks could train on their field stoves. The troops could also practice eating out of mess kits and cleaning them by dipping them in a series of boiling-hot trash cans of soapy water and rinse water. Believe it or not, it worked. The officers did have it a little better in that each company had an officer's mess kit with stainless steel plates, cups, and tableware. Plus, a separate mess tent would be available with tables and chairs. The mess detail got to clean up after the officers.

On the particular day in question, J. Lamar and his XO had just finished a big breakfast of greasy eggs, bacon, and SOS. (If this acronym needs explaining, you have been living under a rock.) On their way to get the training day started, they stopped by the latrine to wet down some cigarette butts. As they opened the door, they immediately discerned that someone had brought his food in the latrine, placed it on the bottom of a turned-up trash can and apparently proceeded to use one of the holes. Talk about an urgent call to nature.

The culprit had to be an officer because it was a stainless steel plate from an officer's mess kit. J. Lamar looked at the XO, the XO looked at J. Lamar, and they both looked at the plate of food sitting in the middle of a latrine.

The XO, being one who spoke his mind without the fear of attribution or even retribution, asked out loud the burning question, "What drunk SOB would bring a plate of food into a shit house?"

From within the stall came the curt reply, "This drunk SOB would." The unmistakable voice belonged to the battlegroup CEO/commander, a short, feisty full colonel. At this point, the sphincter muscles of J. Lamar and the XO tightened so the need and desire to wet cigarette butts ended. They beat a hasty retreat from the latrine in hopes that the colonel, with his mind occupied on more pressing matters, did not recognize them. It did give them a good tale for the other young officers in the battlegroup. Could you feature this happening in a civilian corporate setting? No way!

You Inspect What, When?

As you know, all good eating establishments must have a good manager or chef or, in the military, mess sergeant. J. Lamar's company had such a person, Sergeant First Class James Leroy Beam. You're right; he went by Jim Beam and consumed copious amounts of the product by the same name.

SFC Beam, like his supply sergeant, wall-busting, drinking buddy SSG Ready, served in the Korean War. He said he moved mess halls up and down the Korean Peninsula like a yoyo. Also, like his drinking buddy, SFC Beam had a quick temper which he used effectively when required. Woe be to a KP (kitchen police) who left grease on a pot or pan. He had been known to throw the pot or pan at the guilty individual. Didn't take too many such incidents to ensure the cooking utensils were cleaned properly.

One of the favorite tales told by SSG Ready on SFC Beam involved a retrograde movement in Korea, otherwise known as retreating like hell. Seems that SFC Beam had set up his mess hall alongside the withdrawal route to feed the soldiers on the run. Sort of a forerunner to the fast-food restaurants we all know and love today.

Right in the middle of all this, what would appear but an inspection team from the Division Support Command to check proper cooking and sanitation procedures. These guys were in clean khaki uniforms with pith helmets and clipboards full of inspection checklists. What occurred next was apparently not a pretty sight.

The IIC (inspector in charge) determined Jim Beam to be the mess sergeant and approached him to lay out the inspection procedures. Beam listened to the instructions which included directions that the cooks would be lined up for a uniform-and-fingernail-cleanliness inspection; that the various utensils and implements used to prepare food would be neatly displayed for inspection; and that the paperwork showing accountability and control of supplies would also be made available for the inspection team's perusal. Can't you just feature the picture? A pristine clean IIC, standing in the middle of a combat zone, giving these instructions to a disheveled, unshaven, bleary-eyed mess sergeant who had probably been awake for over twenty-four straight hours.

Remember SFC Beam's propensity for throwing pots and pans. Well, this situation, in his mind, called for something equally as drastic. As the reality set in that the IIC was serious and this was not a joke set up by SSG Ready, SFC Beam went into action. The first thing he did was rip the inspection checklist into smaller checklists. Remember that the food preparation implements were to be inspected? One such implement was an eight-inch meat cleaver. He grabbed it and began moving toward the IIC in a rather menacing manner making statements to the effect that he and his mess personnel were feeding soldiers and didn't have the time or the inclination to be inspected by a bunch of REMFs (rear echelon m—— f——).

The IIC and the rest of the inspection team decided that in a combat zone, discretion is the better part of valor in many instances. This was such an instance. The IIC immediately conducted his own retrograde movement out of SFC Beam's arms reach which had increased by eight inches. No official reports were ever filed on the incident but SFC Beam's commanding officer did tell him he would have to be more tactful in his actions toward inspection teams. The slight rebuke was given with a big wink.

This prior history sets the scene for a similar situation which occurred with Sergeants Beam and Ready. During another one of J. Lamar's frequent tours of duty as OG (officer of the guard), one of the guards reported movement and lights in the mess hall of J. Lamar's company. Of course, he had more than a passing interest since he had the extra duty as mess officer for the company. He proceeded to make a quick check to see what was going on.

Not too much to his surprise, J. Lamar found two rather inebriated (drunk to you rednecks) sergeants. You guessed it—Beam and Ready. Seems as though they had been reminiscing about some of their past escapades and decided it was time to conduct a "midnight-fire" inspection of the mess hall. This is what they told J. Lamar as they giggled, winked, belched, burped, and broke wind. Of course, J. Lamar wanted a more thorough explanation of just what constituted a "midnight-fire" inspection and how often one should be conducted. He did this in a very tactful manner, however, not wanting to upset two people who had been known to use a sledgehammer and meat clever to state their positions.

At this point, SFC Beam did straighten up somewhat when he gleaned that J. Lamar took their excuse for being in the mess hall as somewhat valid. He proceeded to explain that periodically, especially when hunger pains hit, he and SFG Ready needed to inspect the working conditions of the stoves, refrigeration, after-hour cleanliness, and assorted other items to ensure the overall efficiency of the mess hall. He further explained it should be done near midnight so the inspection could be done without interruptions. The basic inspection consisted of cooking eggs, bacon, or steak if available, bread, coffee, and all the fixings for a breakfast and consuming the prepared meal.

"Where does the part about fire come in?" J. Lamar asked.

With a gleam in his eye and wink toward SSG Ready, SFC Beam said, "Lieutenant, we have to make sure we are not too drunk so we don't set fire to the mess hall!" Both sergeants thought this was hilariously funny.

J. Lamar knew he had been had. He decided, however, that he could turn this to his advantage. He made a bargain with the two sergeants that in the future he should be included in the inspections which he felt should occur most of the time late Saturday night or early Sunday morning. The two sergeants agreed wholeheartedly and, with more belching, burping, and breaking wind, began breaking eggs.

How to Get to Umleitung or How Lost Am I?

Before departing from Fort Benning, Georgia, on "Rotaplan," the powers-that-be attempted to prepare the soldiers for the change in culture they were about to experience. One facet of this training was a short crash course in the German language.

Now, trying to get some of the soldiers to learn a foreign language was similar to trying to put a wet noodle up a wildcat's nose. Pretty nigh impossible. This lack of success in language training came home in a graphic way to J. Lamar during one early morning alert.

In order to keep all on their toes and to test reaction times, unannounced alerts would be called which usually meant coming at two or three in the morning—that's right—A.M. All the troops would be mustered (another way to say "roused from drunken stupors and other such type situations") and required to load up the vehicles with equipment, weapons, and bodies and deploy to the predesignated battle positions from which to begin a fight with "Ivan the Terrible" or "Herman, the East German."

These predesignated positions also had predesignated routes to them which were traversed in the normal course of training road marches. This allowed all vehicle commanders to be familiar with the routes so all would arrive at the deployment positions.

This all sounds fine and good when you are dealing with sharp bears but J. Lamar had one NCO who was not a real sharp bear. Now he looked like a bear and was harder than woodpecker lips but with a head to match. Enter Sergeant First Class (SFC) Alvis Gustavis Reavis. He didn't do proud by the name.

While moving out during one such alert described above, SFC Reavis became separated from the platoon's column. This was bad. SFC Reavis had the innate ability to even get lost in his own bed.

J. Lamar finally made radio contact with SFC Reavis and attempted to ascertain his location. SFC Reavis being, so he thought, keen of wit and mind stated he had been on a road to "Umleitung" for the last few miles and once reaching the village of "Umleitung" should be easily found. There was one small problem.

Remember the language lessons previously discussed? SFC Reavis had not excelled in these classes. Had he done so, he would have known *umleitung* was the German word for "detour."

Needless to say, J. Lamar did not arrive at the deployment position with his entire platoon. SFC Reavis did finally arrive at a deployment position, only three companies south of his squad's normal position. Some more of the experience gaining we mentioned earlier. At least, SFC Reavis did not strike out on his own toward "Umleitung" during the next alert.

How to Make a Grown Man Cry

Sometimes second lieutenants have to get their pleasure where they can. J. Lamar had had a particularly trying week which culminated in his being the officer of the guard on Saturday night. Now Saturday night at the Baumholder O'Club (O as in officer) during the early 1960s meant a good steak, good booze, and a good floor show. So with these possibilities being held from him because of guard duty, J. Lamar's mood was that of a mad Brahman bull in full heat.

One of the first duties to be performed as officer of the guard was the guard mount inspection. This inspection served a bunch of requirements—got everyone there at the same time, ensured all the troops had the required equipment, ensured all guard personnel were properly briefed and knew the orders of the guard, and most importantly to the troops, the inspection presented the opportunity to vie for the coveted "Colonel's Orderly." Being selected "Colonel's Orderly" meant no actual manning of a guard post. The soldier got to be with the colonel all the next duty day, and, in some cases, it meant a three-day pass to do whatever the soldier desired. So the stakes were high and many of the soldiers really went all out to get themselves all spit-shined and polished from head to toe.

On this particular guard mount, J. Lamar came across a young PFC (Private First Class) who could have posed for a recruiting poster. He really sparkled except for one small area. He had not paid enough attention to the condition of the tongues of his boots. That's right; there was dust under his boot laces.

Being in the mood he was, J. Lamar felt no compassion toward the PFC and told him he had dirty boots. The PFC looked down and could actually see his face reflected in the high spit shine on the toes of his boot. At that point, J. Lamar severely chastised (polite way of saying "chewed his ass") the PFC for the dust. The PFC had no recourse but to fight the urge to wrap his weapon around J. Lamar's neck like a big pretzel. J. Lamar left the PFC looking like a forlorn lover whose girlfriend had just left with the town nerd.

One small bit of stress had been passed along but on reflection a few days later, J. Lamar felt a twinge of remorse over what he had done. Some more of that experience-learning process. He learned not to let petty personal feelings get in the way of proper treatment of people under him.

Being on Guard Mount Can Be Scary

J Lamar did get the opportunity to rectify his rather harsh treatment of one soldier on guard by being a little more sympathetic during another officer of the guard tour of duty. A normal tour of guard duty was from 1800 hours (6 P.M. to the National Guard) to 0600 hours the next morning, broken down into two-hour increments.

Due to the location of J. Lamar's unit, and signs of the times in the early 1960s (the Berlin Wall was less than two years old), guard duty was considered rather serious business. In many cases, especially stateside, guard duty fell under the aura of training more than actually guarding anything of importance. It was believed that having to maintain vigilant demeanor for a two-hour stretch from 2 A.M. to 4 A.M. while walking a guard post around an eight-foot chain-link fence enclosing stacks of concertina/barbed wire would prepare a soldier for the real thing overseas. It also kept a bunch of soldiers out of the bars and off the streets at night.

What occurred during the particular tour of duty in question was not something that could be anticipated to be included in training. As indicated, the sites secured, or guarded, in Germany were usually of importance and did require vigilant demeanor. The soldiers were allowed to carry five rounds of live ammunition to protect themselves, the property or site being guarded, and to sound the alarm if threatened.

Now control of this live ammunition was tighter than a G-string on a Vegas showgirl. Each round was counted out to and signed for by each guard. This procedure took place each time the guards exchanged tours of duty and under the direct supervision of the sergeant of the relief who also had to sign verifying the correct count and exchange. Of course, at the beginning of the tour, the OG had the opportunity to sign for all the ammunition. At the end of the tour, the procedure was reversed.

Woe be unto the officer of the guard who did not have all his rounds. This would be worse than not having all his marbles which, in the case of some of J. Lamar's lieutenant buddies, appeared to be a distinct possibility. Missing ammunition after guard duty would result in an immediate meeting with the colonel—one of those one-sided meetings where the colonel did the asking and ass-chewing while the OG stood at attention answering and quivering.

At this point, it must be stated that one of these type of meetings had never been required. Before an OG or his sergeants would have allowed this to happen, they probably would have broken open their combat load of ammunition stored in one of their platoon's APCs. Missing ammunition from here could be rectified a hell of a lot easier. (Remember the C-ration fiasco?)

On to the trials and tribulations of J. Lamar's OG tour of duty.

One of the young soldiers in J. Lamar's platoon, a PFC Fernando Ramon Antonio Nigal Coronado ("Franc" for short), displayed a great dislike for the dark, in particular, when by himself. Guess where most guard posts are? You got it; they were at night at some remote side of the motor pool. Such was the post PFC Franc had on the night in question.

Part of the duties of the OG is to check each and every guard post once before midnight and once after midnight. Now, an enterprising OG who liked to sleep would check about 2030 hours (National Guard types, figure it out for yourselves) and then about 0400 hours while sleeping in between. J. Lamar was no different than most OGs. He did the split check as described above usually arriving at each post with full beam lights and a loud "How's it going?" Keep in mind that young soldiers with live ammunition did not need to be surprised. J. Lamar had completed his first check and settled in for a night of sleep.

Back to our young guard PFC Franc. The motor-pool post Franc guarded backed up to a heavily wooded area with a deep ravine leading away from the area. Apparently, in times past, garbage and assorted trash had been thrown into the ravine, and it had become a favorite rooting spot for some of the local wild hogs inhabiting the wooded area.

Hunting and/or shooting any wildlife in Germany is under strict control of the local *jagermeister* or game warden. PFC Franc was not aware of nor cared about the rules. He only knew he had the 2400-hours-to-0200-hours shift. This was just about the time J. Lamar had really gone into a deep slumber after assorted dreams and REMs.

As luck would have it, the hogs were out and about. They began their grunting, squealing, snorting, and rooting. Now, for a young person who didn't like the dark, to hear such commotion became an unnerving event. Franc conjured up thoughts and images which to

him looked and sounded like a herd of Tyrannosaurus rexes coming up the ravine. What to do had not been covered in his instructions from the sergeant of the relief nor did any of his general guard orders say anything about an attack from wild animals.

PFC Franc did what most scared-to-death people would do. He locked and loaded five rounds of ammunition and commenced to fire away. At 0100 hours in the morning, a weapon being fired resounds throughout the countryside.

Not only did J. Lamar wake up in a hurry but just about everyone else on post did too, including most of the dogs that commenced to howl and bark. The wild hogs broke and ran squealing back to their safe haven in the woods. J. Lamar knew he had a meeting on tap first thing in the morning.

After learning from Franc what had occurred, J. Lamar spent the rest of the night writing a report to explain away the night's commotion and status of the five missing rounds of ammunition. He even had the presence of mind to secure the five spent cartridges for show-and-tell to the colonel. The meeting actually went fairly well and resulted in new instructions being formulated concerning the handling of wild hogs and other animals while on guard.

Once PFC Franc quit shaking and slobbering, J. Lamar told him not to worry about it and to be assured he would only be assigned to less frightening guard posts in the future. The only real criticism J. Lamar had for PFC Franc was his marksmanship. He wondered why Franc hadn't hit one of the hogs. One could only guess that trying to take good aim while you are about to piss all over yourself is difficult at best.

What Happened to the Rock?

As previously mentioned, second lieutenants took every opportunity to get some pleasure from their low station in life—bottom of the officer chain of command.

The battlegroup to which J. Lamar belonged while in Germany on "Rotaplan" had a command and staff group who liked to work hard as well as play hard. One of the fun things they did each week was to select the junior officer (first or second lieutenant) who had pulled the biggest bonehead act. This officer would then be awarded the "Doofus Award" at officers' call held each Friday. Part of the award, in addition to the public humiliation and shame, included presentation of a large rock which had a picture of the unit's crest painted on it. This rock would then be "proudly" displayed on the officer's desk or work table and also would be carried to all meals, Officers' Club, or any place visited by that officer.

Some awardees became recluses during their week of glory. Others displayed the rock as a badge of some distinction. The rock had to be protected at all costs and returned the next week for presentation to the next "lucky" recipient.

During one particularly trying week of field duty, a double award of the rock occurred.

There is a saying that armor by its nature is offensive, and armor officers are also offensive. The battlegroup had two such armor officers. Lieutenants Harry S. Humphrey (and he had "one"—a hairy ass, that is) and Beauregard T. Ledbetter (yes, he was from Alabama).

In any event, these lieutenants had covered themselves in glory as well as mud by getting their platoons stuck in a quagmire which was represented on the map as a swamp. Ever audacious, these two armor officers plowed full steam ahead.

They received the coveted rock and had to promise they would go everywhere together with the rock prominently displayed.

Being audacious and offensive, Lieutenants Humphrey and Ledbetter were inseparable as well as overbearing the next week while keepers of the rock.

At the next officers' call, the rock arrived late as did the two armor officers—seems as if they had had a mishap on the way out of the motor pool. One of the lieutenants—neither would confess or blame the other—just happened to drop the rock as a tracked vehicle was being parked. The rock just happened to fall in the path of the tracked vehicle and it just happened to get broken into many smaller rocks.

The ever audacious and offensive lieutenants did place the smaller rocks in a sand bag and return them to the officers' call. The command and staff types were chagrined to say the least. The other lieutenants were laughing up their sleeves and envious of the armor types for having the nerve to break the rock.

You guessed it. Lieutenants Humphrey and Ledbetter received a second "Doofus Award" with the mission to secure a replacement rock. They accomplished the mission with much glee and support from their fellow lieutenants. One-upmanship brought to its highest level.

The Five-Man Infantry Squad

The annals of military history are replete with the development of and attempts to develop new and better ways to wage war on the ground and in the air. Sometimes these developments involved equipment and weapons, and at other times, they involved organizations.

Some of the more notable equipment or weapons which impacted the waging of war included the long bow, gun powder, internal combustion engines which led to tanks and airplanes or helicopters, and, last but not least, the atomic bomb. This is by no means an exhaustive list of all the developments.

The long bow gave the British an upper hand against the French at the Battle of Crecy. This allowed Peter and Frances to send Pierre and François packing. Gun powder, of course, eventually made all the close-in fighting tools obsolete (i.e., spears, spikes, swords), as well as the long bow.

With the advent of the internal combustion engine, the face of war took on a very different look. It eventually evolved into what many in Europe came to know and hate—*blitzkrieg* (i.e., "lightning war"). Blitzkrieg massed air forces and mechanized ground forces in swift moving attacks which, in the proper terrain and situation, became very effective. Of course, blitzkrieg could be trumped by the swift use of atomic or nuclear weapons—the ultimate "big rock."

So much for the quick history on the development of "bigger and better rocks."

One of the proposed organizations which died on the drawing board or more exactly at a dining-in was the "Five-Man Infantry Squad." J. Lamar and five of his fellow lieutenants had the honor and task of supplying some entertainment for the battlegroup dining-in.

Now a dining-in, for the uninitiated, is a very formal affair with dress blues, tennis shoes, and a light coat of oil as some are wont to say. Suffice it to say, there are certain rituals and protocol to be observed. One in particular is that a dining-in is all formal up to a point, and then it can become rather raunchy and ribald.

J. Lamar and his buddies, however, saw the dining-in as a way to put forth a serious proposal in a less-than-serious atmosphere in hopes it would catch on. If you believe that, then you would also believe, and would probably buy, all the mountain property along the coast of Florida. The proposal took much thought and planning. The planning sessions were usually conducted while consuming large amounts of German beer and bratwurst.

If the TO&E (table of organization and equipment) for the "Five-Man Infantry Squad" were reviewed, it would be intuitively obvious to the most casual observer that J. Lamar and his buddies were trying to cover a lot of bases.

J. Lamar, as the OIC, made the presentation to the assembled officers and dignitaries at the dining-in. He explained, in detail, the rank, weaponry, and uniform of the various squad members. You say it shouldn't have been difficult with only five members, but you ain't seen a squad like this one—and you probably never will.

The ranking squad member and leader was a second lieutenant. That's right; the most revered (by his own momma), and, yet, the most reviled (by his superior-ranking officer) officer in the U.S. Army. He came fully equipped with two inert hand grenades (You don't really think you would give a second lieutenant live grenades, do you?); a .45 caliber pistol with only one round so he could only hurt one person—most likely himself; large gold bars on his shoulder and shirt collar to let everyone know to steer clear; a whistle so he could amuse himself in a way other than the normal way (you figure it out); and a box of crayons with which to take notes or color in the lines on a map. Of course, having all second lieutenants as squad leaders gave more slots to be filled by all the military academy and ROTC graduates who aspired to be in this infantry.

Every unit worth its salt has a sergeant major. The "Five-Man Infantry Squad" was no exception. Somebody had to look out for the lieutenant. Who better than a sergeant major who had looked out for generals on down? One stipulation was that the sergeant major would have a minimum of thirty years in service. Do you think this would create some quick retirements or what? Of course, some would view it as a way to bone up on hunting, fishing, and beer guzzling. The sergeant major would be unarmed due to the fact that most were

meaner than tanyard Doberman pinschers. The rank insignia on his fatigue sleeve measured about ten inches high and five inches wide. Again, this was done to let people know he was the member of a "Five-Man Infantry Squad" and had a second lieutenant as boss. This alone would have made his disposition less than friendly.

The third squad member carried the super rank of specialist tenth class so all would know he was the most qualified of the bunch. Yeah, right! You could immediately tell how qualified he was by the fact that he wore the steel pot without a helmet liner, carried all his gear in a large Sears shopping bag, and had a telescoping swagger stick as his close-in weapon. It was maintained that the telescoping swagger stick could reach out and touch someone. Ma Bell would have been proud.

Every unit needs at least one private, and the "Five-Man Infantry Squad" was so blessed. The private came with unbloused fatigues, dirty boots; two days growth of beard; missing buttons on the pockets of his fatigue shirt; a dark ring around the sweatband of his field cap; a sling shot around his arm; and smelling like a barn full of wet goats. The epitome of what a private ought to be.

Last, but not least, every unit has a dud. Why not designate a spot and get it over with. The "Five-Man Infantry Squad" was the perfect unit for this. The old saying is that "shit slides downhill." Why not let it end on the dud's head? This could be accomplished in the "Five-Man Infantry Squad." The uniform for the dud was the army's grey sweatsuit but with "DUD" spelled out on the chest vis-à-vis "ARMY." Just wanted to clarify things.

What could the "Five-Man Infantry Squad" do? Not a hell of a lot. What was the "Five-Man Infantry Squad" supposed to do? Not a hell of a lot. What did the "Five-Man Infantry Squad" do? Not a hell of a lot other than provide some comic relief about what might could be.

J. Lamar and his buddies had fun with the skit. The battlegroup sergeant major almost had a coronary thinking of prospects. The senior officer present at the dining-in, a one-star general, directed that all references to the "Five-Man Infantry Squad" be left at the dining-in lest some pencil-necked geek at the Pentagon get hold of the concept and turn it into reality.

Such became the fate of the "Five-Man Infantry Squad."

Where Did You Say the Machete Is?

While in Germany, J. Lamar had the distinct "pleasure" of escorting a brigadier general (one star) ADC (Assistant Division Commander) for a day. This particular ADC had survived WWII and Korea and had been awarded too many medals to count. His countenance (for the non-English majors this means his "expression") resembled that of an eagle about to spear a rabbit with his talons—very focused. He could look straight through a person and, like John Wayne toilet paper, he didn't take shit off anybody.

The ADC quickly perceived that J. Lamar did not wear the ranger tab on his fatigues. The general told J. Lamar he would go to Ranger School on returning to the states after "Rotaplan."

Fifteen days after returning to the states, J. Lamar departed for Ranger School. For the civilian types who are wondering why the hell the army needed a bunch of Rangers—pay attention. Ranger school ain't no school to learn about forest conservation or how to fight forest fires. Army rangers don't take care of forests—they patrol through them at night, trip over dead fall, have bush limbs smack them in the face, and generally remain in a disoriented state most of the time.

In J. Lamar's time, Ranger School consisted of nine weeks of constant patrolling—three weeks at Fort Benning, Georgia, getting in physical shape and learning basic patrolling techniques; three weeks in the mountains of North Georgia near the village of Dahlonega learning how to keep from falling over dead fall and how to avoid the local moonshine stills (these were strictly off limits); and three weeks in Florida on the Eglin Air Force Base Complex learning how to wade in swamps up to the armpits.

By the time the class reached Florida, most of the students had blisters on blisters from walking in the mountains and had lost enough sleep to become zombie-like in appearance. The students had lost their body fat, their sense of humor, and their ability to think straight at all times. In addition, the students were under the daily control of instructors/lane graders who, like truck-stop toilet paper, wouldn't take crap off anybody (must be a lot of people like that in the military).

All ranger students were equal in rank. However, the actual senior in rank was more equal when it came time to carry heavy pieces of equipment like the radio, machine gun, or extra blank ammunition.

J. Lamar, as a second lieutenant, was one of the less equal types. Hence, if not in charge as the patrol leader, he usually had a "prick 25" (portable radio) strapped to his back or an M-60 (machine gun) slung over his shoulder. These items were in addition to his own personal gear and equipment. This is when J. Lamar believed the old adage "travel light and freeze at night."

As mentioned earlier, most of the time in the Florida phase of Ranger School involved patrolling in swamps with armpit-deep water, plus one other attractive feature—fast flowing rivers. These rivers really didn't flow; they ran.

Because of this feature, a standard item of equipment carried on patrols was a nylon river rope. This rope, as the name implies, became a safety feature when crossing the streams.

Upon reaching a stream, the strongest swimmer in the patrol tied the rope around his waist and plunged across, minus equipment, to the other side. After securing the rope on both sides, the rest of the patrol used it as a safety line while crossing. You get the picture.

It was just such a crossing that gave J. Lamar one of his more enjoyable memories of Ranger School. Getting wet in a river enjoyable? Actually the memory was made before the river crossing took place.

One of J. Lamar's patrols had been moving most of the night. By the thickness of the undergrowth, he could tell the patrol was getting close to a river. Sure enough, the patrol stopped, and in short order, the word came down through the patrol to send up the river rope.

No one ever admitted who FUBBed (fouled up beyond belief) by not having a river rope, but the word came back up to the head of the patrol, "We ain't got a river rope."

At this point, the lane grader (remember the truck-stop toilet paper qualities they possess) probably asked the patrol leader, "What do you do now?"

The patrol leader, in a flash of brilliance or mental gridlock, put out the word, "Send up the machete."

J. Lamar wasn't sure if the patrol leader intended to kill himself or try to build a raft. It became a moot point.

Via muffled snickers, the word went through the patrol to send up the machete. As the message got to one student (in real life, a senior captain named J. T. Armbruister with a bad case of CRS—couldn't remember shit), he came out with a loud, "Aw, shit! The friggin' machete is with the friggin' river rope!" At this point, the entire patrol, including the lane grader, rolled in gales of laughter.

The patrol eventually did get across the river. This particular group of rangers had a new saying to break the tension during the rest of the course.

J. Lamar did get the coveted ranger tab and made a point of ensuring that the ADC saw it on his fatigues. He even received a "warm fuzzy" letter from the general which made all the long days and nights worth it. Of course, J. Lamar also had a tension-breaking phrase to use.

Play War Ain't the Real Thing

When J. Lamar returned to his unit from Ranger School, the second thing he did on greeting his wife, Peggy Sue Ann, was to set his rucksack down. (You quick-of-mind types should be able to figure out the first thing he did.) You got to remember that for nine weeks, J. Lamar had been walking through woods, rivers, and swamps with a bunch of dirty, dog-faced, tired, tough, lean, and mean ranger students.

The closest J. Lamar came to a meaningful relationship or release of pent-up emotions (you get the picture) was with snakes or snapping turtles. Not what he really had in mind. In any event, he was home and could release those pent-up emotions.

The third thing J. Lamar did was to tell Peggy Sue Ann the good news about the future (actually the next week) goings-on in his unit.

J. Lamar, along with the rest of his division, was to depart for three weeks on a large scale FTX called Swift Strike, to be conducted across the State of South Carolina. The first thing Peggy Sue Ann wanted to do was give somebody a swift kick in the ass for taking J. Lamar away again. She had some news of her own. Their first baby was on the way and she wanted J. Lamar around to share in the morning sickness and overall cranky mood she was going to be in.

The saving grace for J. Lamar came in the fact that the whole division would be gone, and there were other wives in the battle-group in the same shape as Peggy Sue Ann. Remember the return from Europe and "Rotoplan"? The race was now on to see which couple would have the first "Return from Rotoplan" baby. J. Lamar and Peggy Sue Ann were in the running. They actually came in second nine months later with a bouncing baby girl born on Valentine's Day.

Back to Swift Strike and playing war. This FTX involved four divisions—two airborne, the 101st and the 82nd; one mechanized infantry, the 4th; and one straight-legged infantry, the 2nd (J. Lamar's division). The division was known as the Indianhead Division with the motto "Second to None." The division's patch was a large black arrow shaped with the head of an Indian chief centered in a white star superimposed on the black background. It was a pretty patch.

Due to the fact that the Indianhead Division was quote "straight-legged," soldiers wearing the patch had to, many times, fight their way in and out of bars when the subject was brought up. This occurred a lot around Fort Benning, Georgia, home of the division, because Benning was also home of the Airborne School. In many cases, the airborne students discovered that jumping from planes had nothing to do with fighting ability. In other words, they got their asses kicked by a bunch of "legs."

The "Second to None" bunch had incentive to do good in Swift Strike because they were opposed by the 82nd Airborne—the "All American Division." J. Lamar and his platoon knew that at some point they would go to "war" with elements from the 82nd and would, in all likelihood, hear the epithet "leg" shouted their way. J. Lamar just hoped the "war" didn't turn into a barroom-brawl-type situation.

The platoon, when not walking, did get to ride in open-air two-and-one-half-ton trucks. The old deuce and a half was so "fondly" remembered by many soldiers because of its hemorrhoid-producing ride. In any event, J. Lamar received a mission to take his platoon out to secure an "important" road junction. So off they went.

As they got close to the area of the road junction, J. Lamar stopped his little convoy and sent a recon patrol to check out the area. Actually, he wanted to make sure he wasn't lost. Sure enough, the "enemy" was already there. Another platoon-sized force had set up behind hay bales and was wearing that detested "All American Division" patch. The battle was about to be joined, as they say.

J. Lamar did report to his company commander and ask for mortar fire. Not real, you understand, but play-like so he could say he had wiped out the "enemy." He then deployed his platoon to attack the remnants of resistance left from the mortar barrage. With blank ammo brazing, the attack began. Of course, once the clamor from the yells and blanks woke up the other platoon, their leader countered with his report to his commander for fire support, etc.

J. Lamar's platoon moved through the intersection "killing" all the defenders. Not sure where the hay bales came from but they supposedly represented foxholes. Play-like, you see. At some point, the two platoon leaders got everyone to cease fire and pull back to their own positions. Strangely enough, no real physical confrontation occurred.

J. Lamar and his opposing counterpart, a big West Point graduate, Elwood Perkins, met in the middle of the intersection to sort out what had happened. Neither unit had an umpire with them. That's right, in an FTX like Swift Strike, there are officers and NCOs assigned to act as umpires similar to officials in a football game. They determine, based on the situation, who had the upper hand as to better firepower, better fire and maneuver, better cover and concealment, and generally who "won" any particular meeting engagement.

Just as J. Lamar and his new found lieutenant friend Elwood had pretty well agreed on who did what to whom, up roared the two company commanders with their respective umpires in tow. At this juncture, J. Lamar and "Big El," as he would be known, got out of the way. They told their troops to take a break in place because real battle was about to be joined between the company commanders and the umpires.

The two lieutenants learned a little about each other such as both were country boys and both liked football, Jack Daniel whiskey, and jumping out of airplanes. Little did they know that they would both make a career in the military and be assigned together to the language school, Special Forces, and ultimately end their careers serving in the same organization. Also, little did they know that J. Lamar's comment, "You know, this play war ain't the real thing," would change in less than three years. They found themselves in Vietnam where it wasn't "play war" anymore. It was the real thing.

You Are Where? Doing What?

Now J. Lamar and all the other soldiers from four divisions did survive the "play war" of Swift Strike and the heat, chiggers, mosquitoes, swamps, and snakes of South Carolina. They returned home as conquering "heroes" because everybody wins in a big FTX like Swift Strike—so the umpires say.

Once again J. Lamar went through the setting down his rucksack ceremony with Peggy Sue Ann. By this time, he had become rather dexterous at it. Little did he know they would go through this ceremony many times in his career. Seems like his assignments placed J. Lamar in units which stayed in the field most of the time.

After a few days to clean equipment and complete POM, J. Lamar's division had a few days of stand down. This was a time to renew acquaintances with wives, kids, and girlfriends (for the single types); eat something that didn't come from little olive drab-colored cans; sleep in a bed; take long, hot showers; and ride in vehicles that didn't produce hemorrhoids or jar your eyeteeth.

Unbeknownst to J. Lamar and most of his unit, they were about to receive training on another type of transportation—boats. "The army has boats?" you ask. Some, but not the type involved in amphibious landings used extensively in World War II and Korea. They were going to Little Creek, Virginia, to train in amphibious operations—learn how to work with the navy, if that's possible. So once again, they packed up their weapons and equipment and took a long (approximately 750 miles) convoy from Fort Benning, Georgia, to Little Creek, Virginia, at approximately twenty-five to thirty miles per hour. This was before interstate highways. Suffice it to say, it was a tiresome, butt-numbing trip.

Once J. Lamar's unit unpacked and set up camp, as it were, in the middle of a naval base, training came at a fast and furious pace. Much physical training to keep the troops tired (not to mention J. Lamar and his fellow lieutenants) and to get prepared for the infamous Pre H-hour transfers and amphibious landing assaults.

These transfers mentioned above had to do with transferring from one bigger boat ("ship" to naval types) to a smaller boat to eventually transfer to even smaller boats, known as Mike boats or Peter boats. These smaller boats were then used to transport troops to the beaches or somewhere close to beaches for the amphibious landings. Sounds rather simple, doesn't it?

Well, trying to climb up and down the cargo nets hung over the sides of boats with all your equipment and weapons strapped on your back ain't the easiest thing to do, more particularly if the seas had any kind of swells, which they usually did. The smaller boats would ride up and down on the swells, which caused the cargo nets to either be as tight as a G-string or limp as an octogenarian bridegroom.

Another problem faced by the army troops involved getting use to living on a boat. Below deck, where the troops were housed, was hot, cramped, and smelly. With the canvas sleeping cots being no more than thirty inches apart and stacked three deep, calling it close quarters was an understatement. If one soldier got seasick, then be assured those within smelling distance would do likewise. It spread faster than a rumor in an all-girl dormitory.

Maybe there was a method in the living-quarters madness. The soldiers were ready to go anywhere to get out, even if it meant climbing up and down cargo nets and making amphibious landings.

Finally, the big day arrived, and the great amphibious operation for J. Lamar and his fellow soldiers began. It was considered a success for his platoon because they all finally got ashore with no one drowned and only one weapon lost. Not bad, considering the fact that J. Lamar's boat got stuck on a sandbar about one hundred meters offshore and they had to wade through chest-deep water. J. Lamar made a memo to himself that if ever given the choice, an amphibious landing would not rank high as a preferred method to wage an invasion or attack.

The units finally dried out, cleaned their weapons, and removed sand from their boots and crotches. Then guess what they were about to do. That's right, make the long convoy back to Fort Benning, Georgia. One small difference. The senior officers and commanders were to fly back and the junior officers were to ride back and be in charge of the convoy. It's called RHIP (rank has its privilege), or gaining experience, depending on one's perspective.

J. Lamar was placed in charge of his company's portion of the convoy. He did get to ride in a jeep with a radio. This would be good except for the fact that the overall convoy commander was a rather shaky, senior captain from the battalion staff. Prior to departing for Fort Benning, the captain had a long-winded briefing and covered every little nit-picking detail two times over. In particular, he went over the radio call signs and reporting procedures to determine each unit's location and rate of march, or present vehicle speed. And it had better be within the speed guidelines set for the convoy (i.e., twenty-five to thirty miles per hour). The call sign system was very simple—use "volleyball" plus the phonetic sound of company letter (i.e., A—alpha, B—bravo). The captain's call sign was Hotel since he was from the headquarters staff.

Finally, the convoy departed. All went well until the captain began requesting status reports about every fifteen to thirty minutes. He would go through the whole routine with each company (i.e., "Volleyball Alpha, this is Volleyball Hotel. What is your present location and rate of march? Over."). There was no abbreviated form of reply allowed, such as: "Hotel, this is Alpha, located near (closest town) at twenty-five miles per hour. Over." The reply had to be: "Volleyball Hotel, this is Volleyball Alpha. My present location is (closest town) and my present rate of march is twenty-five miles per hour. Over." Then, the captain would repeat the entire transmissions to verify instead of just: "Alpha, this is Hotel, Roger, Out." Periodically, the captain would also pull off the road to check vehicle intervals (fifty meters between vehicles) and determine if the correct rate of march was being observed. Give some people a little authority.

This radio harangue continued the entire trip back to Fort Benning. J. Lamar finally grew tired of the constant status reporting and made his final report when about thirty miles outside Benning. After receiving the standard request: "Volleyball Alpha, this is Volleyball Hotel, etc., etc."

J. Lamar came back with: "This is Alpha, I'm somewhere in the state of Georgia, going like a bat out of hell. Out!" and proceeded to turn off his radio. He and his driver began laughing at what the captain probably looked like trying to figure out the answer.

They later learned from the other company lieutenants that when asked by Hotel their status, they answered with a rousing: "We're in the same situation as Alpha, Out!" Oddly enough, the requests for status reports ceased at that point and nothing was said after all the units pulled into Benning.

Peggy Sue Ann did ask J. Lamar what "Volleyball Alpha" meant. Seems for a night or two after getting home, J. Lamar talked in his sleep.

The Air Force Does It Again, But Wrong

Another one of the fun schools J. Lamar requested to attend involved training in special warfare operations in preparation for an assignment to Special Forces—otherwise known as the "Green Berets." This particular school also consisted of physically, as well as mentally, taxing training conducted at the lovely post Fort Bragg, North Carolina. Notice the fort is spelled with two Gs and is named after the Civil War general, Braxton Bragg. But by surviving the Special Forces training or even a tour of duty with the 82nd Airborne Division, also stationed at Fort Bragg, one could expect to brag about it.

One incident of particular note during J. Lamar's special warfare course came as a result of the U.S. Air Force. The last big FTX of the course involved an airborne operation in which the students parachuted into a national forest in the middle of North Carolina. Once on the ground, the Special Forces A-Team, to which J. Lamar belonged, would join up with a "guerrilla" force to put into effect all they had learned in the classroom.

The planning for the airborne operation included a map study of the DZ (drop zone) which revealed a small lake off the southeastern end of the DZ. (Remember this location.) One of the student team

leaders, First Lieutenant Anthony Joseph Massarelli, known as Tony Joe, could not swim very well. So it was decided, based on the direction the plane would be flying (from the south to the north), that Tony Joe would jump out last from the side of the plane which put him over the northwestern end of the DZ. This would preclude any possibility of Tony Joe getting near the lake on landing. Good planning!

But Murphy's Law (you know, if something can go wrong, it will) took over on the night of the jump. After the air force crew had been briefed and given direction of flight to the DZ, the team loaded up and waited for the green light to exit the aircraft. One small problem developed—an engine caught fire and the plane had to return to the airfield. Not to worry, there was a standby crew and plane waiting.

Not real sure, and it could not be proved, but the replacement crew must have had their supper (for you Yankees, that's southern for dinner) in the bar. They took off after a brief orientation and unbeknownst to the team, proceeded to fly the route to the DZ in reverse.

You got it. The plane came in over the DZ flying in the opposite and wrong direction (from north to south). The pilot apparently thought the DZ had been set up backwards but still signaled the jumpmaster (the person who controls and gets the jumpers out of the aircraft) to give the "GO!" command.

Now for the sharp-of-mind, keen-of-wit people who have been paying attention, you already know where Tony Joe came out of the plane—on the southeastern edge of the DZ near the lake. To him the lake appeared like the Atlantic Ocean and he could only climb so high up the webbing and suspension lines of his parachute. Fortunately, the wind carried him away from the lake into the trees. To Tony Joe, tree limbs breaking his fall were a hell of a sight better than water.

You might imagine the confusion and disorientation of the team as a whole. The assembly plan worked okay but it took a while to convince everyone that their compasses were not showing the wrong direction.

Of course, the air force crew flew off into the night thinking they had done a good job. They are lucky the team couldn't get to them.

As can be imagined there were numerous comments made about the crew's family and heritage, not to mention the many ways their anatomy would have been rent asunder if the team could have gotten to them.

Don't Break the Cookies

After successfully completing the special warfare school and surviving the air-force fiasco, J. Lamar ended up back in Germany with his first Special Forces assignment. The 10th Special Forces had its headquarters in the lovely Bavarian town of Bad Toltz. (*Bad* in German ain't like *bad* to a red neck. In German, it means "bath" or "spa" as in a resort-type meaning.)

Anyway, J. Lamar arrived in the dead of winter and immediately took over a Special Forces A-Team. An A-Team consists of twelve members, two officers and ten NCOs (remember these are the folks who protect officers and keep them out of trouble). The team was in the middle of cross-country ski training. You guessed it. J. Lamar had never been on a pair of skis and he showed it. Trying to ski with a sixty-pound rucksack and weapon strapped on his back made J. Lamar look like a humped-back camel walking on ice. Once he fell (which was often), J. Lamar then looked like a turtle on its back trying to get up. He did, with the help from his team NCOs, become pretty proficient on skis.

Remember the alerts J. Lamar had gone through during the "Rotaplan" tour to Germany a few years back? Well, the 10th Special Forces had them, too. Except during the Special Forces alerts, all the team's equipment and supplies to include C-rations (those succulent meals packed in tin cans) had to be loaded on trucks which would then transport the team to an airfield for simulated airborne operations.

During one such alert, the team was fast and furiously loading the truck which included throwing the cases of C-rations to the front of the truck bed.

On the scene appeared Major Donald Ulysses Douthit (yes, his initials do him justice as an apt description). In his best command voice, the major shouted for J. Lamar's team to stop throwing the C-rations. When asked by one of the team's NCOs (a Korean War veteran whose disposition was also like truck-stop toilet paper), "Why the hell for?" the major replied, "Because if you throw the C-rations, you might break the cookies." At that point, J. Lamar thought it best to direct the major to the other side of the parking lot in order to keep his team from rendering him bodily harm.

However, after all calmed down, another rally cry had been adopted for team situations which were not going just right, "Don't break the cookies!"

The Dangers of Cross-Country Skiing

The C-ration-loading incident was not the first exposure for J. Lamar and his team to Major Douthit (a.k.a. Major Dud). No, they had been privy to some of his innate wisdom prior to commencing winter training, in particular downhill and cross-country skiing.

Now you might ask if skiing could be considered appropriate training for the military. Seeing how many people spend buckets of money going to such places as Vail, Aspen, Switzerland, and many other places around the world that have snow, slibovitz, and sensuous women on the slopes, yes it was. It must be clarified that the ski-training areas for the 10th Special Forces only had snow on the slopes (wink, wink).

Ski training is appropriate for Special Forces in certain parts of the world due to terrain and climate conditions (i.e., Europe). Infiltration of a Special Forces team/unit could be accomplished in one of three ways—dropping in from the sky by parachute, coming in from the sea by small boat operations, or coming in overland with walking the principal means. However, in many cases, especially in winter, coming in on cross-country skis is the best option. Hence, the ski training.

"Why then the downhill-skiing training?" you ask. At some point in the early years of forming Special Forces type units in Europe, a ski lodge in the Bavarian Alps was appropriated from the German government for use by the unit as a "safe house" in the rescue training for future contingencies to exfiltrate (opposite of infiltrate) downed U.S. and Allied Air Force pilots. Sounds good, doesn't it? The fact that the lodge was located in one of the better ski areas had no bearing on the selection process (wink, wink). The natural evolution of things led to the annual ski training being conducted by the units of the 10th Special Forces.

While some of the 10th trained in downhill skiing, the rest trained in cross-country skiing in the lower elevations and then they would rotate. As previously mentioned, J. Lamar joined the 10th just as the ski training began. If you think he had problems on cross-country skis, you ain't seen nothing 'til he got on the downhill slopes. He really got "on" them. His whole body became one huge snowplow as he attempted to reach the ski lodge. He spent more time getting up from falls than skiing. Of course, he made up for his lack of skiing prowess by his ability to down copious amounts of German beer and bratwurst at night around the lodge fireplace.

As with all good military training, safety on the slopes was stressed. In some cases (i.e., J. Lamar), the best safety approach would have been to leave the individuals home. Another aspect to be considered was the equipment issued by the U.S. Army. Remember, the items were low-bid and standardized where one size fits all as much as possible.

Especially cumbersome and not the newest types were the cross-country skis. They were wider, longer, and made of heavier wood than many of the civilian types. The bindings which held the foot on the ski did not have up-to-date release mechanisms. If the ski wanted to go a particular way, it took the leg and foot with it, which made for some uncomfortable rides. The skis also were reinforced on the edges with metal strips.

Enter Major Douthit and his safety lecture wisdom.

This particular year had not been a banner year for snow at the lower elevations. In any event, cross-country training would go on. And with the training came the safety lecture. Now you would think a bunch of senior NCOs and company-grade captains and lieutenants would not be required to receive such a briefing. These briefings are usually reserved for privates and specialists and the dangers of driving, drinking, and dipping their "wicks" in the wrong places are covered.

Major Douthit harangued the gathered assembly about the vicissitudes of the ski slopes. He emphasized how skiing into trees, partially submerged boulders, or other skiers would be detrimental to one's health, not to mention the wear and tear that would result on the outdated ski equipment. At this point, the major made mention of the obvious lack of good snow in the lower elevations resulting in many bare spots which one could not ski across. He further stated that in order to keep from injury, one would have to show diligence while carrying skis across these bare areas.

With this comment, a crusty sergeant major, a World War II veteran, asked the burning question, "How would you get injured walking across open ground while carrying skis?"

The major pulled his rotund body to its fullest height and stated in a condescending manner, "Why, Sergeant Major, you could cut your neck from the edge of the skis if not careful." Why the major thought of that danger no one will ever know because no more questions were asked. They all just wanted to get through with the briefing before anymore such "dangers" of cross-country skiing were pointed out.

Overrun by Viet Cong Ducks!

In short order, J. Lamar's tour of duty with the 10th Special Forces in beautiful Germany ended. In its place came a tour in Vietnam with the 5th Special Forces. You talk about culture shock! From the peaceful Black Forest to the black hole of Southeast Asia in about a month's time.

J. Lamar and one of his good buddies from the 10th, a Captain C. T. Henry, ended up in the same general location in III Corps due west of Saigon. Now C. T. (never did know what his initials stood for)

had a body build that could be considered unique. He was so thin, he could stand sideways, wink an eye, and look like a needle.

As an introduction to Vietnam, J. Lamar and C. T. accompanied a patrol to figuratively and literally get their feet wet. The area of operations, located in the northern part of an area called the "Plain of Reeds," was covered with knee-to-waist deep water. Every few hundred yards would be a tree square with a bamboo and thatch-roofed hut occupied by Vietnamese.

At one such tree square, only the old grandfather was present, along with a hut full of baby ducks. No full head count was taken but J. Lamar and C. T. estimated about two or three hundred. When asked where everyone else was, the old grandfather replied, "All in Saigon selling rice." Yeah, and if you believed *that* he had some used Cadillacs for sale parked out back.

At that point, the far tree line opened up with fire. J. Lamar and C. T., along with the rest of the patrol, took cover behind a berm, returned fire, and called for artillery. Just as the firing all ceased from both sides, out of the hut and over J. Lamar and C. T. came the baby ducks in full charge and chirping at the top of their lungs. C. T. didn't take too kindly to being overrun by Viet Cong ducks. He took out his bayonet and clipped off the heads of a few before they fled in full retreat back to the hut.

J. Lamar had a great temptation to call in a body count of fifteen Viet Cong ducks KIA (killed in action) but C. T. cocked his head to one side and said it would be better if he didn't. J. Lamar relented but frequently reminded C. T. of the baby duck attack.

Did You Get the Luncheon Meat?

One of the major problems for some Special Forces teams in Vietnam was resupply of food. Depending on which U.S. regular units were located nearby or how often a team could send someone to the rear to scrounge for food determined how well they ate. Being a new team in a new camp caused J. Lamar's team to be on short rations a few times. One time in particular, due to bad weather and the lack of a good scrounging mission, J. Lamar's team went almost two weeks with nothing to eat but chili con carne, rice, and french bread laced with cooked weevils. There are not too many variations on how to prepare chili and rice. You can put rice on the chili or chili on the rice; you get the picture.

Once the weather turned better, J. Lamar sent one of his team members (a New York Yankee type) Sergeant Edward Dineno (Eddie D) to get some food for the team. Eddie D had shown the ability to scrounge equipment so it became axiomatic (told you he was a Yankee) that he could do the same for food. Eddie D was successful and sent a radio message that he had a case of luncheon meat on board the chopper and asked if someone could please have the jeep waiting to pick him up. Of course, he had other supplies which were all loaded on the jeep and taken to the team house.

One small glitch. After all the supplies were unloaded, there was no case of luncheon meat—only a large case of X-ray film. Seems as if Eddie D had loaded the wrong case off the loading dock. The team didn't have an X-ray machine nor did they know how to cook X-ray film.

Remember the "Doofus Award" J. Lamar encountered in Germany? He had instituted a similar award in Vietnam. It was a weekly ritual which "honored" the best blunder for the week. Eddie D won it hands down for his case of X-ray film "luncheon meat."

Each award was illustrated as a cartoon by the team executive officer, Lieutenant Bruce Ashley. Don't let the name fool you because his initials, BA, did him proud. He could be a badass. Anyway, he depicted the "Doofus Award" for Eddie D as Eddie sitting in a latrine (that's French for "outhouse") eating boxes of X-ray film and shitting cans of luncheon meat. It was never determined what happened to the luncheon meat or where the X-ray film belonged. Suffice it to say, Eddie D did not go on food-scrounging missions after that incident.

The Great Barge Chase or How Do You Lose a Boat That Big?

As indicated previously, J. Lamar and his Special Forces team were in the middle of building their new camp. Because of the wet terrain and high water table in the "Plain of Reeds," the camp's bunkers and various other buildings had to be built above ground. In order to save time, J. Lamar and an engineer buddy of his struck upon the idea of using CONEXs (containers exchange) as the basic inside structure for the bunkers.

CONEXs are large metal "boxes" used to haul and store cargo. They are large enough to stand in (unless you are a center in the National Basketball Association) and have double doors for easy access. J. Lamar had firing ports for machine guns and other weapons cut in the sides. These bunkers were then sandbagged for additional protection. One last improvement was to put a concrete cap over the sand bags. It made the bunkers look like a portion of the French Maginot line or the German implacements above the beaches of Normandy.

One small problem developed. Sand was hard to come by. The initial sand had been flown in by helicopter in the swing-loaded CONEXs. The containers could only be loaded about one-third full because of the weight involved. This was not cost effective.

The camp was located on a canal which had been constructed by the French during their stay in Vietnam. This canal ran into the Vam Co Dong River which eventually made its way to the coast and the open seas. The river, as well as the canal, was affected by the tides each day. Remember this point.

J. Lamar had requested a barge load of sand through supply channels but he was not holding his breath while waiting for it to arrive.

At this point, a savior in the form of COMUSMACV (Commander, United States Military Assistance Command, Vietnam, General William C. Westmoreland) came to J. Lamar's camp for a briefing. Part of the briefing dealt with the construction of the bunkers. As an afterthought, J. Lamar casually mentioned the sand problem and that he had requested a barge of sand. Now, you have to understand COMUSMACV did not travel alone as he went about the countryside of Vietnam. A number of folks, some euphemistically known as "horse holders" (a throw back to the cavalry days), came along to take notes and apparently react to comments made by COMUSMACV. He had stated that someone would look into the request for sand.

Lo and behold, a week later a message came down that a river barge of sand would arrive at J. Lamar's camp. Miracles never cease; it arrived on a high tide and was tied securely (so J. Lamar and his team thought) to palm tree stumps along the canal bank.

The next problem (so they thought) was how to unload the barge. That night, while all was quiet and unloading plans were being devised, the tide (I told you to remember this) began to go out. Guess what went with it? You got it—the barge load of sand.

J. Lamar had reported earlier to his headquarters that the barge had arrived. He now had to report it had departed under the cover of darkness and with the tide.

A barge chase operation was immediately mounted in engineer boats with forty-horsepower outboard motors. Not knowing how long the barge had been gone, J. Lamar had no idea where or how far it might have gone. He knew having to answer the question "How do you lose a barge?" would not be easy, particularly if asked by COMUSMACV. Hence, the recovery chase.

By the time the operation began, it was already past midnight. The forty-horsepower outboard motors were not the quietest around so the whole "neighborhood" knew they were coming down the river. After going approximately four miles down the river and not sighting the barge, J. Lamar turned his "armada" around and headed back to camp.

As he reported no luck in finding the barge, he thought he could hear laughter in the background at the headquarters communications center. It was no laughing matter to J. Lamar.

He did request a "bird dog" (small single-engine observation plane) for first light to fly over the area to see if the barge was anywhere to be found.

Talk about your good luck. What the tide takes away, it can bring back. The "bird dog" spotted the barge coming slowly up the river. The barge chase crew mounted their boats once again and sure enough found the barge drifting up the river with the tide.

J. Lamar tied two of the engineer boats to the barge and slowly but surely brought it up the river, made the turn into the canal, and finally got it back to the camp.

After securely lashing the barge to the remains of a bridge as well as the tree stumps, J. Lamar was able to report the return of the barge. He also reported that the camp's radios would be turned off because he and the rest of his team were going to have a "Return of the Barge Party" (i.e., they were going to get drunk, walk on their knees, and puke straight up).

J. Lamar never found out if COMUSMACV was made aware of the "Great Barge Chase." By the way, they finally had to resort to the old bucket routine to unload the sand. Took awhile, but it worked and the bunkers looked good.

Reel in the Chicken

Sometimes when left to come up with entertainment, the American soldier can be very innovative. However, J. Lamar's team received one-upmanship from none other than a monkey.

The monkey's name was Nummy. Not sure where the name came from but suffice it to say, Nummy had had his share of trials and tribulations. For some reason, he had been castrated. Also, one of his hind legs had been broken and had healed crooked causing him to walk even funnier than normal.

In any event, Nummy was playful and was allowed out of his cage on a chain. The camp had a resident guard dog by the name of Corporal Studley. Corporal Studley gave Nummy wide berth because anytime Studley got near, Nummy would attempt, and sometimes succeeded, in jumping on his back for a ride. Looked something like a small jockey on a runaway horse at the Kentucky Derby.

One of the NCOs thought it would be fun to tie a chicken to Nummy's chain. In no time Nummy developed a real liking for the chicken who then became the object of his rides around the camp. (It was not, however, to the chicken's liking.) Nummy also saw fit to pluck feathers from the chicken. As the mood struck, Nummy would "reel in the chicken" and in his inimitable style have his "way."

This was a source for a lot of laughs for the team. However, it backfired on J. Lamar one day during a visit to the camp by a female contingent from the USO (United Service Organization) out of Saigon (otherwise known as "Donut Dollies").

As he was conducting the group on a tour of the camp, J. Lamar had the misfortune of approaching Nummy and his chicken friend just as Nummy became playful. The contingent's reaction went from (before Nummy reeled in the chicken) "Oh, what a cute monkey!" to "My God, what is he doing?" J. Lamar could only try to divert their attention to the bunkers, or mortar pits, or somewhere other than Nummy. He hustled them on out to the chopper pad and sent them on their way.

Of course, other team members had observed the incident. J. Lamar was not allowed to forget. It also sparked a new battle cry for the team—"Reel in the chicken!"

What Not to Do If You Have Hemorrhoids

The TV ads are full of solutions to that age-old problem known as hemorrhoids. However, J. Lamar "found" a solution through an inadvertent act on his part.

GI ("Guvmint" Issue)

After carrying eighty-pound rucksacks through waist-deep water, J. Lamar developed a very swollen, sore, tender case of the old hemorrhoids. Now, there was no local Super D drugstore nearby the camp from which J. Lamar could procure Tucks, Preparation H, or such cures. Even his team medics did not have a readily available elixir (fancy way of saying "cure") for his problem. He finally made his way back to the rear (no pun intended) and an appointment at the clinic.

After the preliminary paperwork, J. Lamar found himself in a waiting room. The doctor came in, asked the perfunctory questions (I mean who could be excited about looking at a swollen anus), and then had J. Lamar drop his pants and get upon the examination table face down.

At this point, things went downhill for J. Lamar. The doctor gave the usual "uh huh" and then asked J. Lamar to exert pressure in his anal area as he would while having a bowel movement. J. Lamar took him strictly at his request and proceeded to, as they say, cut a fart of which any red-blooded male would have been proud.

Not sure who was more surprised—the doctor or J. Lamar. In any event, the doctor immediately cleared his throat and declared, "We are going to have to cut on these."

To which J. Lamar replied, "I'm sorry for breaking wind in your face but I hope that is the only solution."

The doctor replied "That's the only solution. See you in OR."

J. Lamar could never be sure if the doctor was sincere or just vindictive. Suffice it to say, he was cut on the next day. He promised himself if ever placed in a similar situation, he would exert a little more self-control.

By the way, the doctor also gave J. Lamar some pills which he stated would make the first bowel movement a little less painful. If trying to shit an unpeeled pineapple backwards is a less painful feeling, then the pills worked.

There Will Be No Counting

Having survived ducks, barges, monkeys, and even hemorrhoids, J. Lamar returned from Vietnam to Fort Benning, Georgia (that Queen of Battle home), to attend IOAC (Infantry Officers Advanced Course). This course consisted of about six months of classes crammed into nine months.

It was a time to renew acquaintances both with fellow officers and families. The commandant in his opening remarks to the class of approximately two hundred infantry captains stated that about 99.4 percent of the class had served in Vietnam and at the conclusion of the course 99.4 percent would return to Vietnam. So the commandant told the class to relax, have fun, and learn what they could. Of course, the class wanted to know which two officers (the .6 percent) had not yet been to Vietnam.

The IOAC course consisted of all types of classes but in particular tactics and logistics. For the uninitiated, logistics encompasses the getting, maintaining, and moving of beans, bullets, and all the things people use in waging war. In many of these classes, a very important point to be made by the instructor would be prefaced with comments to the effect that if the students didn't remember the point or how to apply a particular facet of tactics or logistics, they would surely die in Vietnam. Now, you must remember 99.4 percent of these students had already survived a tour of duty there.

One of J. Lamar's classmates, a rather crusty captain by the name of Jimmy Lee Lewis (no relation to the singer), took issue with one such situation by blurting out a resounding "48, 49, 50,—some shit!" right in the middle of class. This was an instant hit and became the class battle cry for similar such remarks made from the instructor platform. Some instructors took it good-naturedly because they, too, had been there. Some, having been forewarned, threw out a roll of toilet paper when confronted with the class battle cry.

But, as in any situation, there are those who did not appreciate the humor intended. The class received a verbal warning from the student battalion commander, a crusty old lieutenant colonel who had a personality similar to a bag of dust—real dry. The warning was that there would be no 48, 49, 50s sounded off in unison by the class during periods of instruction.

Now, Jimmy Lee did not mind creating problems for instructors by asking sharp-shooting questions or by making side comments which could be heard for a twenty-foot radius. He even had signs which he would hold up during class for his classmates to see saying "applause," "hiss," "boo," or "laugh." To say Jimmy Lee was a rebel is a classic understatement. As he stated, "What the hell they going to do? Send me back to Vietnam?" Made sense.

After being told no more 48, 49, 50s by the battalion commander, Jimmy Lee did not give it up. His next battle cry became "51, 52, Screw you!" As you might imagine after the class used this battle cry a day or two, another meeting was called by the crusty old lieutenant colonel. It became evident to all in the class, particularly Jimmy Lee, that there would be no more counting of any description. The colonel did show a little humor of his own when he stated very succinctly (for the farm bureau types, this means "concisely") "53, 54, you will count no more!" And you know, the class didn't.

God Is Alive and Well

Once the counting in class stopped, the day-to-day tedium set in. However, the boredom was overcome one particular afternoon through a set of most unusual coincidences.

At the time, the army had not been using ADP (automated data processing) that long. In particular, not many of the infantry types even knew what ADP meant. Some thought it was some type of atomic demolitions.

On the day in question, an ADP class was scheduled for the afternoon and, more particularly, a Friday afternoon. Some of the class had decided to get an early start for the weekend and had consumed beer for their lunch. Some it made sleepy; others it made rowdy. J. Lamar fell in the rowdy bunch.

The class started innocently enough by an instructor from the army's ADP center at Fort Benjamin Harrison, Indiana. He, however, had one major strike against him. He was a leg (means "non-airborne/paratrooper qualified") AG (adjutant general) officer. The AGs are the personnel officer paperpushers of the army. They are not held in high esteem by infantry types unless they hold the key to school quotas or R&R (rest and relaxation) trips. In any event, the young captain was giving it his best to a bunch of uninterested, sleepy, somewhat inebriated ("drunk" for the farm bureau types) students.

In order to show the real worth and capabilities of the ADP process, the captain put a picture of a 35 mm slide on the screen in front of the class. He then asked the class, "Would you believe the entire New Testament could be microfilmed on a single 35 mm slide?"

Enter J. Lamar as Brother Leroy, a Southern Baptist preacher-type character. J. Lamar had been known to get rowdy and lapse into Brother Leroy at various social functions, particularly after having had a few rounds of drink.

As the captain finished his question, J. Lamar, who surprisingly had been paying attention, jumped up and shouted in his best Brother Leroy voice, "Yes, I believe!" The instructor, to say the least, was caught off guard, but he figured that at least the class was now awake.

This is where the coincidence came into play from one of the students, Captain James "Hopalong" Cassidy. "Hopalong" sat down front in the amphitheater-type classroom. As J. Lamar, now performing as Brother Leroy, came out with, "What are the preachers going to do when the devil is saved?" "Amen!" "Hopalong" stood up, faced the class, unbuttoned his fatigue shirt and revealed a T-shirt with the following statement printed on it: "God is alive and well in Mexico City!"

At this point, there was mass pandemonium in the class. The young AG, leg captain used his microphone cord as a noose and made it appear he had hung himself. He very wisely put the class on break for a few minutes.

Another class cry had been formed: "God is alive and well!" The rest of the ADP class became one of the better received periods of instruction.

When "Hopalong" was asked why in the world he had on the particular T-shirt, he replied his wife had been out of town so no laundry had been done. He had worn all his clean underwear and T-shirts save the God-is-alive-and-well shirt. No one asked to see his underwear and he didn't volunteer to show it.

A Defense Counselor's Nightmare

Believe it or not, upon finishing the IOAC, J. Lamar remained at Fort Benning. He became commander of a one-of-a-kind unit in the U.S. Army—the Scout Dog Training Detachment. This particular unit, as the name implies, had the mission to train scout dogs as well as their handlers for assignment to Vietnam. More of this later.

As a unit commander and by this time a young major, J. Lamar had the distinct pleasure and duty of being assigned to a special court-martial board. These boards are usually comprised of five to seven members who are usually commissioned officers.

The board sits as judge and jury to conduct court-martial hearings for transgressions committed by soldiers as set forth in the "Red Book" or manual for court-martials. The book or manual is also known as the UCMJ (Uniform Code of Military Justice). Some folks might call the phrase "military justice" an oxymoron. ("Oxymoron," in case you were wondering, is putting words together which appear to be contradictory.) There is, however, justice in the military.

One of the most prevalent transgressions committed by soldiers is that of AWOL (absence without leave). Soldiers get homesick, fed up, or screamed at and decide to depart their unit without prior approval to do so. If the AWOL goes on too long, it can be classified as desertion.

Enter PFC (Private First Class) Arthur Lee Wilson. As you have guessed by now, Arthur Lee had gone AWOL, had been returned to his unit, and had received a special court-martial. J. Lamar was selected to be a member of Arthur Lee's court-martial board.

To ensure that proper procedures are followed, the government's case is presented by a lawyer (trial counsel) from the JAG (Judge Advocate General office) and the individual being court-martialed is represented by a lawyer (defense counsel) also from the JAG office.

The court-martial board hears both sides of the story and then makes a determination as to guilt or innocence. In most AWOL cases, the decision is a "slam dunk," as they say. If a soldier ain't present and ain't got a reason for not being present, then he is wrong.

Once guilt is determined, the court-martial moves into the mitigating and extenuating circumstances phase. This is the phase in which the defense counsel earns his pay. He brings up those factors which will hopefully result in a lighter punishment for his "client."

In Arthur Lee's case, the defense counsel attempted to show Arthur Lee had been a good soldier through testimonies of character witnesses such as his squad leader, his platoon sergeant, and some of his fellow soldiers. But the main mitigating circumstance the defense counsel used dealt with why Arthur Lee went AWOL in the first place.

Arthur Lee was married and went AWOL to get a better paying job in order to make enough money to bring his young wife to live with him in the Fort Benning area. This picture of Arthur Lee as a good family man was a plausible approach and might have worked but for one small glitch.

Arthur Lee's best friend, Jimmy Leroy Ledbetter (no kin to Beauregard T. Ledbetter), was put on the witness stand to verify this story and also to prove that Arthur Lee had stayed in the Fort Benning area. The questioning of Jimmy Leroy was going well until the defense counsel instructed Jimmy Leroy to, in his own words, tell the court how he could verify Arthur Lee's whereabouts. The answer given was not the answer wanted or expected.

Jimmy Leroy proceeded to state he had informed the company first sergeant (top NCO in the company) that Arthur Lee was still in the Fort Benning area. At this point, the defense counsel asked, "And just where was Arthur Lee living?" hoping to get the answer "living in Columbus, Georgia." (Columbus was the city next to Fort Benning.)

Instead, Jimmy Leroy answered, "He were at his girlfriend's house."

At this point, the trial counsel ducked his head, Jimmy Leroy slapped his hand over his mouth, the defense counsel rolled his eyes and looked up at the ceiling, Arthur Lee looked like he had been kicked in the stomach by a mule, and the court-martial board had to restrain themselves to keep from laughing. The president of the board, an older lieutenant colonel, called for an immediate recess, cleared the hearing room, and along with the rest of the board had a good laugh.

Needless to say, Arthur Lee did not get to bring his wife to Fort Benning, and with his stockade time, did not get to see his girlfriend for awhile. The defense counsel no doubt learned a good lesson on coaching witnesses. The court-martial board had a good story to tell at happy hour.

What Daylight Savings Time Does to a Schedule

As previously indicated, J. Lamar commanded a special unit involved with training scout dogs and their handlers for assignment to Vietnam. As the name implies, scout dogs were used to seek out the enemy through their acute senses of smell and hearing. The handlers, in essence, "read" their dogs' reactions to smell and sounds while out in front, or point, with a unit on search-and-destroy operations in the jungles of Vietnam. The dogs were not attack dogs or sentry dogs. (The idea will be discussed later.)

The training program for the handlers was a twelve-week course which consisted of basic dog obedience but mainly of patrolling operations in a field-training setting to gain experience of how to "read" the scout dogs. Some of the student dogs went through the course as many as three times before they were shipped to Vietnam. It was not that they were slow learners; instead, it was based on replacement requirements in the some twenty-two scout dog platoons deployed to Vietnam. The dogs did not rotate at the end of a year's tour but stayed for the duration. In other words, it was a one-way trip for the dogs.

As with all good commanders, J. Lamar had frequent meetings with his staff of instructors and support personnel. During one particular Friday afternoon meeting, he wanted to ensure the cadre was briefed on the upcoming change to daylight savings time. At this time, daylight saving was a rather new concept and J. Lamar did not want the problem of cadre and students not being on time to start the next week.

The last item on J. Lamar's briefing notes involved daylight savings. He put out the word, with tongue-in-cheek, that at 0200 hours on Sunday morning everyone should remember to get up and set their clocks forward one hour. He immediately saw a hand shoot up. The less-than-astute cadre member asked, "Do you mean I have to get up to set my clock forward at 0200 in the morning? Can't I set it forward before I go to bed?"

J. Lamar answered, "Yes, you can set your clock ahead anytime you desire over the weekend, but there had better be no one absent from the normal 0530 Monday morning reveille." As an afterthought, J. Lamar stated that the 0530 reveille would actually be 0430 by the sun.

At this point, he could tell a large number of the cadre were confused. He restated that Monday's reveille would be 0530 by the clock but 0430 by the sun. Immediately, a hand shot up followed by the question, "Do you mean we have to be in an hour before reveille?" J. Lamar knew he had opened a can of worms with the "by the sun" remark but decided to have some fun.

"No, reveille will be at the normal time it has always been, 0530 but 0430 by the sun." Eyeballs still were glazed over and an immediate hubbub arose over the fact of having to come in at 0430.

J. Lamar gave a loud, "At ease!" "Now, listen up," he roared. "Set your clocks ahead one hour sometime this weekend. Show up at reveille by the clock at the normal time of 0530 Monday morning which will be 0430 by the sun! Do you have any questions?"

No one moved until the mess sergeant (the NCO in charge of the dining facility and feeding the troops) asked the burning question, "Will we have breakfast at the same time as usual or an hour earlier?" At this point, J. Lamar, along with a large part of the cadre, could no longer hold his laughter. He had not counted on the innocent remark of 0430 by the sun creating such a stir.

As J. Lamar ended the meeting and dismissed the cadre, he wondered how many absentees there would be on Monday or if breakfast would be served early. As it turned out, the first sergeant made sure reveille and breakfast came off without a glitch.

At future meetings, it became a standing routine that one of the cadre would ask if an announced event would be by the clock or by the sun. It always got a laugh.

Scout Dogs Are Not Trained to Attack
(or So J. Lamar Thought)

As previously stated, scout dogs, unlike sentry dogs or guard dogs, were not trained nor expected to use their innate ability to bite or attack the human body. Not that sometimes during training bites did not occur.

J. Lamar had the distinction of reporting the number of soldiers on sick call for dog bites during the brigade command and staff meetings. He also had the distinction of having to report AWOL dogs. When this occurred, an all-points search was conducted to bring the dogs back. The government would be liable for any bites from the AWOL "soldiers," albeit a canine type.

The Infantry Center had three ready-made show-and-tell stops: Airborne School, Ranger School, and the Scout Dog Detachment. The Airborne School, of course, depicted the training of soldiers learning to jump from perfectly good aircrafts. Ranger School depicted soldiers being trained to survive and operate in the wild almost like animals. Scout dog training depicted the training of dogs to become almost humanlike in their actions. So the circle came full, almost.

In any event, during one of the show-and-tell briefings for a member of the Secretary of Defense office, J. Lamar as the BIC (briefer in charge) stated more than once that scout dogs are not trained to nor do they attack as part of their military mission.

As the distinguished visitor was escorted from the dog obstacle course to the patrolling lane to observe actual movement and scouting by a scout dog team, the entourage passed through an area in which various scout dogs were staked out with fifteen-foot chains fastened to trees. With some 450 scout dogs on site at any one time, not all were housed in a kennel. The stake out areas were kept clean by the student soldiers who also fed and watered the dogs as well as groomed them.

As J. Lamar led the visitors, which included the Secretary of Defense representative, the Brigade Executive Officer, the Infantry Center Chief of Staff, and various other "horse holders" and "strap hangers" through the stake out area, he inadvertently walked too close to one of the staked-out dogs. As stated, the dogs were not trained to

attack but the dogs were very protective of their areas, especially if they were not familiar with the person intruding into their space who also did not have food and water. Such was the case with J. Lamar.

Before J. Lamar knew it, he had a 120-pound German Shepherd attached to his left leg at the calf. Exhibiting great self-control and presence of mind, J. Lamar commanded a loud "NO!" which was the command given for scout dogs to stop doing what they were doing. Fortunately, the scout dog broke off the "attack" and the entourage moved on giving wide berth to the stake out areas. (The BEO, Brigade Executive Officer, J. Lamar's immediate boss, almost went into hysterics at the incident.)

J. Lamar moved on as if nothing had happened and his leg was not hurting like hell. The rest of the briefing/tour went without any further incidents. All were impressed with the scout dogs' demonstrated abilities.

Unbeknownst to J. Lamar, the "biting incident" had been observed by the kennel NCOIC (noncommissioned officer in charge) Sergeant Dewey Otto Goforth. You got it, the acronym for his name spells DOG. Where but in the U.S. Army could this happen. Rest assured the NCOIC was never called Dewey.

By the time the VIPs had deported, the word had spread that the major had been "attacked." This is one time the RHIP (rank has its privilege) status did not hold true. J. Lamar, in future briefings, continued to state that scout dogs are not trained to attack but would if given an opportunity. Sergeant "DOG" didn't let J. Lamar forget it either.

Train the Dogs to Do What?

As with any school or training unit, new ideas and innovations are always developed. The Scout Dog Training Detachment was no different.

For the keen-of-eye and sharp-of-wit, the fact that scout dogs needed a handler to "read" the dogs' alert meant the handler had to be in close proximity. This proximity involved a leash usually six to eight feet long. This put the handler close to the action in many cases since the scout dog team, as previously stated, accompanied the patrols up at the point or head of the unit moving forward.

Hence, the idea of training dogs off leash came about. Training the dogs to alert was basically the same on or off leash. As long as the dogs remained in sight all was well. Now, to overcome the out-of-sight problem gave impetus to the development of the off-leash signal collar.

The technique involved strapping a signaling devise on the dog which would emit signals that could be received by the handler equipped with a basic squad radio receiver. The dogs would be signaled by the handler with arm and hand signals when in line of sight or by the silent dog whistle when out of sight. Sounds simple enough, doesn't it?

Enter the "guvmint" and its procurement system. We all have heard of the seven hundred dollars hammer or coffee pots or similar such items. How about a signal collar costing seven hundred dollars per item which proved to be totally worthless? "How did this happen?" you ask. Let J. Lamar tell you.

With the idea of off leash established as feasible, a contract was issued to develop a collar which would emit signals as the scout dog moved over the terrain. Their "beep, beep" signals would then be received by the handler through the squad radio receiver. When the dog stopped to alert, the signal would become a steady "beep." The handler would then move forward to determine if the scout dog had actually alerted or if the dog was taking a "pit" stop.

Believe it or not, J. Lamar received two hundred collars at seven hundred dollars each before the prototype could be field tested. Do you detect what was about to happen?

The collars were strapped on the dogs and the dogs sent to scout. One small problem. The signal remained a constant "beep" even though it was obvious the dog was moving. The collars were tested by shaking to prove that a "beep, beep" signal occurred.

One collar was dismantled to reveal that the signal occurred when a ball of mercury in a small tube moved from end to end which made contact with a sensor and emitted a "beep." When the motion stopped, the ball of mercury settled in one end and resulted in the constant "beep." Good so far, right?

No matter where the collars were placed on the dogs, no "beep, beep" signals were received. J. Lamar and his cadre could not come up with a solution.

A call was made to the company's (which will go unnamed) field representative and the problem described. "Not to worry, we will come down and show you how to operate the collars."

At this point, J. Lamar's patience wore thin as he told the rep, "We know how the collars are supposed to work but when placed on the dogs, nothing happens."

When the rep arrived, he stated he wanted the roughest terrain available so he could show how well the collar would perform. So, away to the boonies they went.

The rep shook the collar to make sure the signal switch was working. (Nothing profound so far on his part.) Then he strapped it around the test dog's neck. (Still nothing profound.) He instructed the handler to send the dog out to scout. (Still nothing profound.) He, along with J. Lamar and the cadre, observed the dog moving over the rough terrain and could hear the constant "beep" being received.

At this point, the rep did something profound. The rep stated in very authoritarian tones a fact which was intuitively obvious to the most casual observer, "The dog is not moving correctly to properly activate the signal switch."

To which J. Lamar replied, "No shit, Sherlock." To say J. Lamar was hot under his fatigue shirt collar would be a classic understatement.

The handler, as instructed, recalled the dog. The rep shook the collar to again ensure the switch worked, and it did.

There ensued a rather pregnant pause which the rep broke by making the startling disclosure that the switch was developed in a lab by using a rocker arm which moved at a certain rate and distance in order to move the mercury in the tube. He asked as an afterthought if it would be possible to train the dogs to move in a similar manner.

At this point, J. Lamar basically came unglued and made remarks to the effect that he had been involved in goat ropings, log cuttings, turkey screws, barn burnings but nothing as fouled up as this adventure. He called it the classic FUBAR situation (i.e., "fouled up beyond all recognition").

Needless to say, the collars were put on the shelf in the supply room. J. Lamar rendered a report on the field rep visit to brigade headquarters. As far as he was concerned, the "guvmint" had been had. In the future, where similar situations received play in the media, J. Lamar had a little better insight as to how a piece of equipment might cost a lot and not really do the job.

It reaffirmed his belief that, in many cases, if you want a piece of equipment developed, tell the average "GI" what you need and it will be developed at a fraction of the cost and will work.

None the Wiser or What's in a Name?

After surviving dog bites, dog AWOLS, and other assorted hazards of command, J. Lamar found himself assigned to the Presidio of Monterey, California for a year of language training at the Defense Language Institute. Believe it or not, this was the second year of language training for him.

The first year had been in the Czech language which is about as far removed from his Tennessee twang as one could get. J. Lamar had fun speaking the language with a southern drawl. Didn't do much for his grades or the nerves of the native instructors. It did, however, teach him a lot more about the English language than he had imagined. You have to know one to be able to learn the other.

The second language was about 180 degrees from Czech. It was Vietnamese. Forty-seven weeks of learning to speak in a singsong voice about five octaves higher than normal. Now for a redneck hillbilly with a natural deep bass voice, this was no easy task. Why the army thought a hillbilly ought to learn such dissimilar languages remains a mystery. But J. Lamar gave it his best shot.

It was during the Vietnamese training that J. Lamar and his fellow classmates took full advantage of a set of circumstances. What resulted was a real play on words.

The Vietnamese word for miss or a young unmarried girl is "co" as in coworker, cohort, or coordinate. You have the picture. As indicated, the instructors at the language school were native to the country of the language they taught.

As you may have gleaned by now, this language training prepared J. Lamar for another tour of duty to Vietnam. Knowing where they would end up after graduation gave the students a reason to be less than serious in many cases. Might as well have fun before the "real" fun began.

In any event, one of the young native instructors had been transferred to the Presidio from Fort Bliss, Texas. During the early stages of the Vietnam conflict, the U.S. Army conducted short orientation courses in the Vietnamese language at Fort Bliss or as some of the more hard rock NCOs called it "Veeatemaknees."

This particular young instructor happened to be single and female. It should be added she was rather attractive as well. She immediately told all the students how well she liked Texas and all things Texan. The students, being quick of wit, seized the opportunity to call her "Co Tex." She thought the nickname was great, the students thought it hilarious, and the more knowledgeable Vietnamese faculty members, wise to the American ways, did not let on about the play on words. No real harm was done and the year of training passed by a little easier.

It Takes How Many BUFEs to Load a Plane?

After completing the Vietnamese language course, J. Lamar, believe it or not, departed for Vietnam and his second tour of duty. Unlike the first time around, however, this time he could at least order a meal or understand the peddlers in the villages.

For his second tour, J. Lamar ended up in the Central Highlands as an advisor to the Vietnamese rangers. In actuality, the ranger battalions were Special Forces (Green Beret) camps which had been converted. The conversion consisted primarily of changing the color of berets from green to maroon and reducing the advisor teams from a twelve-man Special Forces A-Team to a four-man team. It was all part of the process of turning the conduct of the war over to the Vietnamese.

J. Lamar's immediate superior had graduated from the University of Tennessee two years before J. Lamar. He was Major Timmy Mike Jenkins, entrepreneur extraordinary which means he would buy, sell, trade, and bargain for anything from argyle socks to zebra striped pants. Rest assured he always did it for profit but also be assured all the deals were honest and aboveboard in most cases.

One deal, however, almost turned sour. During his first tour, Timmy Mike had operated as a Vietnamese battalion advisor in an area that had a ceramic factory which, among other items, produced ceramic BUFEs. Now, "What the hell is a BUFE?" you ask. As indicated, BUFEs are ceramic. The acronym, BUFE, was coined by some unknown GI, I'm sure, and means "Big Ugly Frigging Elephant." That's right, those green or white or multicolored ceramic elephants you see holding up pieces of glass as coffee tables in someone's den or sitting beside a chair as an end table are BUFEs. They usually come with a good price tag as well.

Timmy Mike, being a sharp dealer in such items, struck upon the grand idea to contact the factory which had been allowed to remain open even during the conflict. He felt he could resale the BUFEs to fellow Americans who, in turn, would ship them home to wives, girlfriends, or family. The plan moved very well and Timmy Mike contracted to buy a "herd" of BUFEs, sixteen to be exact.

One item which presented a problem involved transporting the BUFEs from the factory to Timmy Mike's base of operation. The road network in Vietnam was none too secure as you might have guessed. Enter one army aviator ("pilot" to you civilians) who wanted a BUFE for his wife. He agreed to fly the "herd" of BUFEs in his small fixed-wing army airplane. Maybe not completely legal, but other supplies were included on the load. One of the local army doctors had some bandaids brought in.

The BUFEs were picked up and brought to the Tan Son Nhut Airport in Saigon. The "herd" was loaded on the plane, an eight-passenger plane known as an Otter. One small problem developed. Some of the "herd" had to be placed in the aisle between the seats. A fact not previously mentioned is that a BUFE, like its real counterpart, is rather heavy. The army aviator knew he had a weight distribution problem, but what the heck, he would be taking off on a runway which handled PanAm jumbo jets everyday. Plenty of room.

After being cleared for takeoff, the plane, with the "herd" of BUFEs aboard, lumbered down the runway, and it lumbered, and it lumbered and it bounced a time or two. At this point, Timmy Mike began to feel just a little uneasy like he could see the official report trying to describe how an army aircraft crashed on takeoff at Tan Son Nhut Airport loaded with an unidentified pile of ceramic on board.

The plane lumbered some more and finally after bouncing a few more times, did, slowly but surely, leave the ground just high enough to clear the fence and trees at the very end of the runway.

The pilot very nearly crapped his pants, Timmy Mike went into a near state of shock, and the controllers in the tower were probably one finger push away from calling out the emergency vehicles.

As they say, all's well that ends well. The rest of the flight came off without a hitch. Timmy Mike got rid of his "herd." J. Lamar even bought a pair. Every time he sets a drink down on one of his BUFEs, he is reminded of the almost tragic loss of the "herd."

It might be added that Timmy Mike got out of the BUFE business. He ended up in things considerably smaller and lighter like knives, daggers, and swords. It is understood he is doing quite well.

But They Won't Grow—Maybe It's the Dirt

Nicknames and practical jokes are integral parts of the American society. The U.S. Army, being a slice of this society, had its own brand of ribald nicknames and practical jokes. Hang on, and you will get the gist of what ribald means.

Assigned to the same headquarters as J. Lamar and Timmy Mike was a major with a name and hobby which opened him up to the brand of army humor mentioned above.

You wonder sometimes what mommas and daddies are thinking when they name their kids. They oftentimes don't look ahead to the situations they ultimately create for their offspring. In this particular case, the major's last name was Head and his first name was Richard.

The more astute of you have already gleamed the nickname given to him. You are right—Major Dick Head. Hard as he tried, no one ever called him Richard. So, he suffered through his career known as Major Dick Head.

As previously mentioned, the major practiced a hobby while in Vietnam which drove him crazy trying to figure out the problem and gave his fellow officers a measure of fun, albeit somewhat "tainted" (you will understand the choice of this word later). The hobby involved trying to grow various types of flowers in order to beautify the compound where they lived.

The flower bed happened to be located between the club and the living quarters. (You say, there was a club in the middle of a combat zone? Yes.) In any event, Major Head had his family send him a variety of flower seed. He planted the seed and nurtured them into seedlings. About this time (no one knows for sure who came up with the idea) all of Major Head's fellow officers began "watering" his plants at night on their way from the club to their living quarters or "hooches."

Surprisingly some of the plants flourished, but for the most part, the flowers took on a rather pathetic look. Major Head could not determine the cause even though he received numerous possible reasons from his fellow officers. One, a big red-faced man with the last name of Doody, and, yes, a first name nickname of "Howdy," volunteered that the dirt sure looked different. He should have known. Because, in keeping with his drinking propensities, "Howdy" probably "watered" the flowers more than anyone else in the compound.

No one ever actually told Major Head what the real problem happened to be. After awhile, the nightly "watering" became less funny. The flower bed did survive and added a touch of color and home to the compound. However, Major Head remained Dick Head.

Tricking the Major or
How to Build Esprit de Corps

Believe it or not, folks in the military are given the opportunity to continue their formal education while on active duty. In some cases, the additional schooling is directed by DA (Department of the Army). In other cases, the individual applies for various programs at civilian institutions, and, if selected, becomes a full-fledged student. J. Lamar did just that.

He applied for a program known as ADPRID (Advanced Degree Program for Instructor Duty). In this program, a person, if selected, attends a university to complete an advanced degree with a follow-up assignment at the university in the ROTC Department (remember this is where J. Lamar got started).

Being a big football fan and more particularly an SEC (Southeastern Conference) football fan, J. Lamar applied for assignment to any school in the SEC area. With his first choices being the Universities of Tennessee, Alabama, or Georgia, J. Lamar figured each place would afford him many enjoyable fall Saturday afternoons of spirited games.

Enter the big fickle finger of fate. Using the standard lingo of DA, "due to needs of the service," J. Lamar's assignment was to an SEC school—Vanderbilt University in Nashville, Tennessee. This did place him close to home and would give him the opportunity to watch visiting teams from around the SEC come to town for some spirited workouts.

For those who do not follow SEC football, Vanderbilt (a.k.a. Vandy) always puts up a gallant effort but year in and year out falls a little short against the rest of conference. It may have something to do with the athletes who are recruited and who are able to qualify for admittance. Vanderbilt is known for its academic programs.

This created no small amount of apprehension for J. Lamar. As you may remember, he received his undergraduate degree at the University of Tennessee (a.k.a. the Big Orange, UT, Volunteers, or Vols). The academic differences between UT and Vandy could best be stated that a person attends UT and matriculates at Vandy.

The differences at UT/Vandy football games could be stated by the cheers. UT uses the old standbys of "Rip 'em up! Tear 'em up! Give 'em hell, Tennessee!" "Go Big Orange!" "Defense, Defense!" "Hit 'em a lick harder!" and others that might be banned in Bible-belt Nashville.

Vandy followers, on the other hand, are wont to use more esoteric-sounding exhortations. Doesn't that sound like a Vandy grad speaking? Some of the Vandy cheers are "Fight Fiercely, boys!" "Make them relinquish the ball, Vandy!" "Impede their progress!" and "Score with e'lan!" The one used by Vandy students to show their real distaste for UT is "Nothing sucks like a Big Orange!" Remember the orange connection.

With the aforementioned differences of spirit and approach to football, it must be stated that Vandy basketball is another story. The team usually acquits itself well in the SEC. Strangely enough, the fans and students become as wild-eyed and fanatical as the Big Orange football followers. This setting gave J. Lamar a real lesson in how creative and inventive the Vandy students could be. More particularly the ROTC students.

One of J. Lamar's duties while an instructor in the Vanderbilt ROTC Department was to oversee the color guard. This particular small group of ROTC students, usually two color bearers and two guards, participated at major functions, such as basketball games, by presenting the colors in pregame ceremonies. As everyone knows the colors (usually the U.S. flag along with the school or sometimes the Tennessee state flag) are marched to the center of the gymnasium and presented during the playing of the national anthem. This is done in military fashion with sharp-looking uniforms, snappy marching, crisp movements, and all decorum due the ceremony.

Enter the Vanderbilt Army ROTC Color Guard during a Vanderbilt–University of Tennessee basketball game. J. Lamar had checked the color guard (so he thought) prior to the ceremony to ensure the cadets had the proper uniforms and correct commands. This was the big home game of the year and with the fans already at a fever pitch, J. Lamar wanted the color guard to perform well.

Did they ever!

Between the time J. Lamar left the color guard in order to get to his seat and the actual presenting of colors at mid-floor, the cadets modified their overall appearance ever so slightly but very noticeably. The two cadets who were the "guards" for the colors impaled, or as a UT grad would say, stuck, oranges on the muzzles of their weapons. It was not immediately noticed by J. Lamar until the color guard approached center court. The front rows of the Vandy student section noticed the oranges about the same time.

After one of the more rousing renditions of the "Star Spangled Banner" by the Vandy student section, the color guard proceeded to march over to the edge of the court and then along in front of the student section. By this time, the students were giving the color guard a standing ovation. J. Lamar wanted to give them a swift kick in the ass but his leg wasn't long enough. He did, however, meet them as they came off the court. To say he was displeased is an understatement. It became abundantly clear to the color guard that they had better never display oranges again.

However, this particular incident was outdone the next year during the UT game by the new color guard. This time J. Lamar inspected the uniforms thoroughly (so he thought) and stayed with the color guard until they began their march to center court. Weren't no oranges on the weapons this time.

Part of the color guard uniforms were shiny chrome helmets known as "Chrome domes." Underneath the chrome domes were the standard army-issue olive drab helmet liners. Out of the way and not seen, right? The cadets had a surprise.

After the presentation of the colors and national anthem, the color guard marched to the edge of the court, halted, faced the student section, and with a free hand removed their "chrome domes." In large orange letters, they had spelled out BEAT on the front of their helmet liners. They executed an "about, face" and on the back of their helmet liners had spelled out VOLS.

The student section, along with the major portion of the Vandy home crowd went wild. J. Lamar went wild but for a totally different reason. He knew he had been had. Deep down he admired their ingenuity and had to agree it brought out the crowd's spirit.

The color guard didn't get J. Lamar the next year because he had departed Vanderbilt and Nashville on a new assignment. However, during the next football season, Vandy did beat the Volunteers. As quickly as some of the Vandy ROTC students could get to a telephone, guess who got a phone call? Again, J. Lamar had to admire their spirit and effort in getting in touch with him.

Apparently, his fervor for "the Big Orange" had rubbed off on the Vandy students in their support of the Vandy teams. Not a bad legacy to leave.

The Big Put Down

All the military services have various schools to which their members are sent in order to bring them up to date and prepare them for future assignments. These schools also provide the opportunity to meet contemporaries who will share these future assignments. They also provide some good family time.

One such school is the army's CGSC (Command and General Staff College). This year-long course is conducted at Fort Leavenworth, Kansas.

The first rule at Leavenworth is not to pick up hitchhikers. "Why?" you ask. Because also located in and around Leavenworth are various penal institutions such as the army's disciplinary barracks or DB, the Leavenworth Federal Penitentiary, and both Kansas State men and women's penitentiaries. Hence, the rule.

J. Lamar used his year at CGSC for an additional reason beyond those cited above. All who had attended CGSC stated it was the best year of their life. After a fashion, it became the best year of J. Lamar's life.

By the time J. Lamar reached Leavenworth, his family consisted of one wife (Peggy Sue Ann—yes three names), three kids (Nellie Lenore, Hattie Louise and Junior—all southerners have a Junior) and one dog named Trooper. J. Lamar and Peggy Sue Ann felt this was a tidy number.

The second phone call J. Lamar made, after calling post housing, was to the urology clinic to set an appointment for the big "V" (as in vasectomy) operation. He volunteered to be "fixed." (He hadn't learned yet that you don't volunteer for nothing.)

The date for the big event was set after the necessary counseling sessions and pre-brief by the surgeon. J. Lamar didn't think it was such a big deal because, having been raised on a farm, he thought he knew most of the ways to be "fixed." Little did he know.

The big day arrived and J. Lamar drove himself to the appointment. (First mistake in a long series of mistakes.) As the preparations began, J. Lamar laughed to the urologist/surgeon that, "This must be a type of poetic justice because I helped castrate pigs, lambs, and calves while growing up on a farm." (Second mistake.) The surgeon, being from the streets of Chicago, stated he had no idea how to castrate an animal. This gave J. Lamar no real sense of confidence about what was to take place. The doctor appeared as though his manual dexterity in dealing with J. Lamar's more private parts would leave something to be desired, or, as a redneck would say, "he couldn't wipe his ass with both hands."

However, to take his mind off the situation at hand, J. Lamar proceeded to describe in gory detail the various means used to "fix" animals. He held a seminar, as it were, as he was being "fixed." Anyway, the time did pass rather quickly.

J. Lamar, now fixed and still under the deadening shot, drove himself to Hattie Louise's swim meet. (Third mistake.) Then, after lunch, he returned to class. (Fourth mistake.) About midafternoon, the deadening wore off; J. Lamar's pants got tighter; and he now understood why the pigs squealed, the lambs bleated, and the calves bawled when they had been "fixed." But as they say, about the only place to find sympathy in this type of situation is between sex and syphilis in the dictionary.

J. Lamar finally got home and applied the ice pack he should have applied earlier in the day.

His ordeal did subside through the next few days as far as the pain went. Then came the long wait for the sperm count check to be done at the local post hospital.

Now they gave J. Lamar a lab slip which stated which test was to be performed but they neglected to provide a container in which to collect the sample of semen. J. Lamar, being a Special Forces type, knew how to improvise. He dumped out Peggy Sue Ann's birth control pills and used the plastic pill bottle. He figured what the hell, she didn't need the pills any longer anyway.

In any event, the big day arrived and J. Lamar collected his sample of semen. He then proceeded posthaste to the hospital to turn in the sample for testing. He was met at the lab reception desk by a pert, young, specialist fourth class female medic.

J. Lamar handed in his sample and made a statement he has no idea why he made and immediately regretted making it. (Fifth mistake.) He stated, "I hope this is enough."

The pert young medic took the bottle, looked at the lab slip, turned the bottle up, looked at the sample, smiled, and said, "Well, Sir, if this is all you can do, it's all you can do!"

J. Lamar nearly ran through the wall trying to get out of the hospital. His misery had not ended, however. Based on the test, his semen was still potent and he had to wait another three weeks to submit another sample.

On this particular day, J. Lamar had determined not to say a word to anyone. He collected his sample and again made the trip to the post hospital. However, this time he was met, not by a pert, young female medic, but by an older grey-lady type volunteer. As he handed in his sample, the volunteer asked him, "What time did you take this sample?"

To which J. Lamar replied, "Hell, Lady, I wasn't looking at my watch; it's difficult enough just to hit the bottle."

After this second put down, J. Lamar vowed and determined he would not come back with another sample. He literally took things in his own hands and solved the "equation" for potency. (This was not a mistake.) Once this "fixing" was completed, the year at Leavenworth became better and better.

The CP (Command Post) Is Located Where?

As previously mentioned, CGSC provides an opportunity to meet contemporaries who are from all the different branches of the army and even from other services. Of course, for an infantryman like J. Lamar, all other branches, be they combat arms (i.e., armor, artillery, air defense) or combat support/combat service are support troops for the infantry.

There are also special branches such as the Chaplain Corps ("preachers" to you hillbillies) and the JAG (Judge Advocate General) Corps which is a high-toned way of saying "lawyer." Yes, the military does have lawyers to perform legal requirements. They oversee the military justice system. Of course, the army had its lawyer jokes like the civilians—such as "What is the difference between a 'possum and lawyer crossing a tank trail?" "There would be tank tread skid marks in front of the 'possum!"

The folks who planned and organized the classes at CGSC did give a little forethought. The students are placed in sections of approximately sixty officers who are further broken down into workgroups of approximately fifteen members each. Would you also believe these workgroups were comprised of some combat arm officers, some combat support officers and even some special staff officers? Made sense to J. Lamar.

Enter workgroup 3, section 11—J. Lamar's workgroup. In every military organization there is a command structure with at least someone designated as the leader—enter LTC (Lieutenant Colonel) Jeremiah Phelonius Cornelius. Now two things need to be noted about Jeremiah Phelonius. He was a lawyer and a southerner from North Carolina. With a name like Jeremiah Phelonius, he had a leg up on most lawyers from the start. And, being from the South, he had a way with words as well as the accent that could melt butter.

Jerry P., as he was called, "ruled" the workgroup by common consent. He was pretty low-key except when discussion centering around tactics came up. At that point, Jerry P. became a war horse. He would wax eloquent in a pontifical manner. Due to these propensities, Jerry P. ultimately was selected as CINC WAR (commander-in-chief of war) for the section.

His great stab at glory came during one of the major map exercises conducted during the course. Each student had to prepare his own solution to various phases of the exercise. Certain ones were then called on to present their solutions as commander for the day.

Jerry P., having been selected as division commander, took the assignment very seriously. He put up his map overlays, arranged his notes, and began his briefing/presentation in a very pedagogic manner (high-toned way of saying "like a teacher").

It became readily apparent that Jerry P. had prepared well but with one "minor" glitch. He stated the CP (command post) would be located just east of the village of Silo. It must be pointed out here that the use of and the ability to read military maps is a prerequisite for the course. It isn't that Jerry P. couldn't read a map, he just didn't do a thorough map recon. (He didn't look at it clearly enough). Had he done so, he would have seen that there were about twenty-five "silos" in the AO (area of operation).

You see, every farmstead depicted on the map had a silo which was represented by a small black circular dot with the word silo printed beside it.

To all the sharp-of-wit, keen-of-eye members in the workgroup, this error became immediately evident. One even tried to help Jerry P. by asking a clarifying question of, "What did you say the map coordinates are for the CP?"

At this point, the instructors asked the more incisive question of, "Which village of Silo?"

There followed a rather awkward period of silence as Jerry P. finally gleaned the error. It was quickly corrected by determining an eight-digit map coordinate. Thereafter, the workgroup had the school solution for locating the CP—"It's east of the village of Silo."

This minor setback did not deter Jerry P. As indicated, he eventually became CINC WAR and wore the title proudly. It is reputed that he is presently in North Carolina fomenting a movement to reestablish the Confederacy.

You Swap the Old for the New or Was It New for the Old?

Upon completion of the best year of their lives, J. Lamar and his contemporaries literally spread out in new assignments all around the world. They were the newest trained CGSC graduates and, as such, would be met with open arms by their new units of assignment. There were commanders waiting with "baited breath" and multitudinous (a "bunch," you ninny) requirements for the new graduates.

Had J. Lamar known some of the requirements and situations he was about to encounter, he might have opted to stay in the hills of Tennessee. As it was however, J. Lamar and his family ended up in the land of beer, bratwurst, and BMWs. That's right, Germany. Having made this move once before when the kids were toddlers and having had to lug seven suitcases of various sizes, J. Lamar put out an edict which stated one piece of luggage per person and each person carries his own.

Now this created a big problem for the female members of the group, two of which were approaching their teenage years (Nellie Lenore and Hattie Louise). Peggy Sue Ann already carried a handbag as big as a suitcase. As for Junior, he sure enough believed the old adage "travel light and freeze at night" because he only wore soccer shorts, T-shirts, and tennis shoes, and if Peggy Sue Ann had allowed it, one set would last all week. Anyhow, they all arrived with their suitcases in tow in the land of the "Dogfaced Soldier"—the Third Infantry Division.

J. Lamar became a battalion XO (executive officer) and had more duties and people to oversee than he could shake a stick at. Remember one other time when J. Lamar came to Germany and was involved in the counting of C-rations? Well, as they say, "What goes round, comes round." Only in this situation counting of C-rations wasn't the problem; it was swapping C-rations that became the problem.

Believe it or not, C-rations do finally get old. Now some folks contend they are old from day one. In any event, the word came down to swap C-rations with a manufacturing date of 1972 or earlier and draw new rations with newer manufacturing dates. Easy to do, right? That's what J. Lamar thought, too. He, along with his S-4 (the battalion supply officer) came up with a good idea and plan—so they thought.

The battalion was scheduled for weapons firing at the beautiful Hohenfels Training Center. One of the few places in the world where a person can stand in mud up to his ass and have dust blowing in his face. You get the picture.

While at Hohenfels, the battalion would feed two hots and a C which means, to the quick-of-wit, two mess-hall (dining facility in the new army) prepared meals, and yes, a C-ration meal prepared by hand on a firing range somewhere.

The plan J. Lamar and the S-4, Captain Wilfred (Good Deal) Grafton, came up with seemed foolproof. They would feed their old C-rations while at Hohenfels and draw newer ones from the German run supply depot. Their thinking was that surely with all the units coming through Hohenfels the supply depot would have up-to-date C-rations. As a matter of fact, J. Lamar's battalion actually had no C-rations with earlier manufacturing dates than 1974. He and "Good Deal" felt they would really update their stock.

The plan moved along with one small glitch. The detail sent to pick up the newly requisitioned C-rations was not fully aware of the plan. All they knew to do was pick up the C-rations. You have to understand, the C-ration detail was not composed of the sharpest "bears" in the woods. As you have guessed by now, the depot had its share of old C-rations and issued these to J. Lamar's battalion. In fact, the battalion ended up with older C-rations than it had to begin with.

Once this was discerned by Captain "Good Deal," he immediately apprised J. Lamar. J. Lamar now understood the feelings his company XO had a few years before when he found out about the miscount on C-rations.

J. Lamar's reaction to this turn of events was similar to a Saturn rocket lifting off at the Cape. He literally landed in the middle of the desk of the little old grey-haired German in charge of the depot. It was intuitively obvious to the most casual observer that J. Lamar had a case of the red ass. (To the boys back home, this meant he was mad enough to stomp a mud hole in someone else's ass and wade it dry.) In very short order, the air was cleared and J. Lamar and Captain "Good Deal" had an understanding with the Depot OIC (officer in charge). No more older C-rations for newer C-rations.

J. Lamar thought this incident had been nipped in the bud so that none of his fellow XOs would know about it. However, the division ADC (assistant division commander) for supply had heard about it. Now this ADC, a BG (brigadier general) named Charlie Wayne Dixon, was hard as woodpecker lips and could render a person into a quivering mass of protoplasm, puke, and piss with a few chosen words and looks. At the same time, he did have a sense of humor.

During the next monthly show-and-tell maintenance and supply meeting he held with all the battalion XOs in the division in attendance, General Dixon asked J. Lamar about his plan to swap old C-rations for the new or was it new C-rations for the old. At this point, J. Lamar had to recount for the assembled group of his peers what had transpired.

Of course, from that point forward, J. Lamar had to contend with periodic offers of a good deal on some C-rations from his fellow XOs.

You Americans Never Learn

After training at beautiful spots like Hohenfels, Baumholder, and Grafenwher, the combined military forces stationed in the ETO (European Theater of Operation) participated each year in the granddaddy exercise of them all—REFORGER (Return of Forces to Germany).

Wait a minute, you say. Weren't there a bunch of forces already in Germany? Yes, but many more residing stateside had missions in Europe if the balloon went up. This REFORGER gave a grand opportunity to exercise POM (preparation for overseas movement) which involved packing up equipment, men, and material to participate with the other units in USAREUR (U.S. Army, Europe).

One of the most trying type of movements was known as EDRE (Emergency Deployment Readiness Exercise). In an EDRE, a unit (usually an infantry battalion) would be selected and given about seventy-two hours to board planes for Europe. Upon landing, the command and staff element would be briefed and given maps and the keys to a big warehouse which housed the POMCUS (Prepositioned Material Configured to Unit Sets). This POMCUS equipment would be used by the unit while participating in REFORGER.

Now you are probably wondering who thought up all the various acronyms (there's that word again) just discussed. Not real sure, but J. Lamar had an idea that some little old man with green eye shades, arm bands, and chalky white skin in the lower reaches of the Pentagon had the job. You know the type—has fluorescent lamp burn.

In any event, J. Lamar and his unit had the pleasure of participating in REFORGER. This particular year in question saw the exercise conducted in the Bavaria area of Germany. This is southern Germany, but no one said "ya'll."

One of the interesting features of a large exercise like REFORGER is that units, especially infantry and armor, are mixed or cross-attached to complement each other in conducting operations. One of the companies in J. Lamar's battalion had a platoon of tanks (four M-60 types) attached. Of course, getting a new/different unit attached created logistical problems for the XO due to different repair parts and fuel requirements.

However, in the case of the tank platoon attached to J. Lamar's battalion, the problems became a little more serious.

REFORGER usually lasted two to three weeks and involved controlled, freewheeling maneuvers by two opposing forces.

On the first night of the exercise, the forces to which J. Lamar's battalion belonged began moving to contact. The tank platoon, attached to a rifle company, began moving forward on a small road. Upon making contact, the tank platoon leader moved his four tanks off the road, side by side to move forward to engage the "enemy."

One small problem. A brief look at the map would have made it intuitively obvious to the most casual observer that the small road was the only high and dry ground. The rest showed up on the map as a bog or, as J. Lamar would call it, a swamp.

Almost immediately, the young tank platoon leader knew things were not going right. Maybe it was the scream over his radio from the platoon sergeant which sounded something like, "What the hell, we're in a frigging swamp! Put this son of a bitch in reverse and get back on the road!"

However, by this time, the weight of the tanks prevented them from going anywhere. As a matter of fact, trying to back up actually dug the front of the tanks in deeper so that the rear end stuck up in the air similar to a mallard duck poking its head underwater.

Early rays of sunlight the next morning revealed a sight to behold—four tanks in mud up to the turret. Getting the tanks unstuck became a major operation in itself. It actually took the rest of the exercise to get the tanks out, not to mention the equipment and men it tied up.

The crowning blow came from a little old German who lived in a nearby village. In his best English, he told the DISCOM (Division

Support Command) commander, "You Americans never learn, you stuck tanks in the same field during the war in 1945."

J. Lamar wondered out loud (with-tongue-in-cheek), "Why weren't we given the AAR (after-action report) on that incident? Sure would have saved some time and trouble."

The look J. Lamar received from the DISCOM commander made it abundantly clear that this was no joking matter and that he best get his ass in gear in trying to unstick the tanks. The little old German's comment still made J. Lamar laugh as he drove off to coordinate getting some tank retrievers.

I Have One Hundred Tanks or Ich Habe ein Hundred Panzers

Once the aforementioned tanks were retrieved and REFORGER ended in a rousing success, the real fun began. All the troops and equipment brought to Bavaria had to be cleaned and returned home. Funny how it is in the scheme of things that this type of mission is left to the XOs. The commanders had fought the battle "brilliantly" and now were anxious to get the hell home.

It fell to J. Lamar and the company XOs in the battalion to round up all the vehicles and troops so they could be cleaned and loaded on trains for the trip home. Believe it or not there was a plan as to where to assemble, where to load the trains, and what time to be there.

J. Lamar had some one hundred APCs (armored personnel carriers) and six hundred soldiers to assemble and load. The load-out point designated for his battalion was the town of Memmingen located about twenty-five miles from the assembly point near the village of Babenhausen. Now, getting this "gaggle" of men and machines to the railhead without MP (military police) support presented J. Lamar a slight problem. He came up with a solution which would have made General George Patton proud.

While the troops cleaned bodies and equipment, J. Lamar drove to the police station in Memmingen. He first asked if anyone there spoke English. Not getting very much attention, J. Lamar, in his best German, stated "I have one hundred tanks coming from Babenhausen to the train station in Memmingen." At this point, three different Polizei (German for "police") stepped forward and began asking, in English, how he intended to do this without interrupting the afternoon rush hour. J. Lamar calmly said, "You tell me."

After frenzied consultation among themselves, the Polizei stated to J. Lamar that they would send escort vehicles to lead the convoy through town to the train station. One stipulation was make by the Polizei. The vehicles would be required to be no more than five meters apart and there would be no stopping until they reached the train station. J. Lamar calmly said, "We can handle that." So ended the coordination meeting.

J. Lamar returned to the assembly area, gathered the company XOs together, and gave one of the shortest movement order briefings ever. Basically he stated that order of march would be A, B, C, combat support, and headquarters with the maintenance section dragging rear. All tracks will be lined up on the road nose to butt at 1430 (2:30 P.M. to the National Guard). Once movement began there would be no stopping unless a vehicle broke down. The XOs asked, "Is that all?"

J. Lamar calmly said, "That's it." So ended the briefing.

Of course, J. Lamar hoped and prayed the Germans showed up, the companies stayed closed up, and that nothing broke down. The movement went off without a hitch.

As soon as the loading out was completed, J. Lamar and his jeep driver, a young black soldier from LA (no, not Lower Alabama), did what all smart Americans in Germany do. They headed to the nearest gasthaus (restaurant) and ordered the biggest "wiener schnitzel" (breaded veal) they could find. Once full, J. Lamar and his driver started the long drive home up the autobahn.

J. Lamar still laughs at the look on the German Polizei faces when he stated, "Ich habe ein hundred panzers."

Where Are All the Spies?

Once J. Lamar had had all the fun he could stand as a battalion XO (actually he was promoted to LTC—lieutenant colonel), he transferred to the big headquarters in the sky, USAREUR—United States Army, Europe. This headquarters, located in beautiful Heidelberg, controlled all the U.S. forces in Europe and also worked with allied forces from Germany, Great Britain, Belgium, and the Netherlands, known as Holland for those more familiar with dikes, wooden shoes, and tulips.

Believe it or not, one of the first requirements J. Lamar worked on once being assigned to USAREUR was a handbook of operational differences between the various allied forces and the U.S. forces. In essence, the handbook pointed out the differences in doctrine, procedures, and most importantly, terminology so that U.S. units coming from CONUS (Continental United States), such as REFORGER units, might be better prepared to operate in the NATO (North Atlantic Treaty Organization) atmosphere.

Now that the esoteric explanation is out of the way, just what did J. Lamar do? He, along with another staff officer, sorted out all the doctrine, procedures, and terminology to point out the differences which might cause operational difficulties. One of the main ways to determine these differences and gain information involved face-to-face meetings with staff officers and commanders from the other Allied forces in NATO.

One such fact-finding trip took J. Lamar to the town of Monchen-Gladbach, the location of NORTHAG (Northern Army Group) headquarters. The staff of this headquarters was predominately British and as such the housing, clubs, and other facilities were run along British lines. The mess, or dining facility at which J. Lamar ate, required coat and tie and had pre-dinner cocktails.

During cocktails one evening, J. Lamar met two rather proper British colonels who saw a good "fish" to regale with tales from their various "postings" (assignments) as the British are wont to say.

Colonel Smythe-Balfour, a very dapper individual with grey hair and clipped mustache, appeared to be the more sophisticated and urbane (pointy-headed way of saying "smooth") of the two. Colonel Rathbone, on the other hand, had the appearance and manner of someone who had been around the block a time or two and who would probably try anything once and do it again if it were good. The type of person who would take the manure ball from a tumble bug, give it an acorn, and put it on the wrong road home.

One story in particular that Smythe-Balfour told on Rathbone, which had an ending that befitted Rathbone's character, involved a hotel fire in Malaysia. Seems as they both had been "posted" to Malaysia without family. While there, Rathbone apparently became "enamored" with one of the local "birds," as the colonels called the ladies of the night.

During one of Rathbone's trysts with the "bird," the hotel caught fire. In the ensuing mad scramble to get out, Rathbone, with the "bird" in his arms, was captured on film coming out of the hotel. The picture hit all the tabloids of England with a caption that Major Percival Rathbone in Her Majesty's service had rescued the young "bird" from the burning hotel. Of course, Smythe-Balfour knew the real story but had never revealed it in the true fashion of a stiff, upper-lipped Englishman.

During dinner with the colonels, J. Lamar did observe Rathbone get back at Smythe-Balfour with a good put down.

After they had been served, Rathbone began by tasting his food and then salting it. At this point, Smythe-Balfour began a discourse that during World War II the Germans were able to spot numerous British spies because of their propensity to taste their food first and then salt it. At this comment, Rathbone immediately stopped eating, took a slow, measured look around the room and then stated to Smythe-Balfour in his best British accent, "I think we are quite safe now."

J. Lamar still smiles when he thinks of the gleam in Rathbone's eyes as he scored one on his old friend Smythe-Balfour.

Selling Hamburgers in Germany

An assignment in Germany for an American family by and large became a good learning experience to see and live in another cultural setting. Of course, the word family denotes children, and children need activities.

Enter the DYA (Dependent Youth Activities), DAC (Dependent Activities Council), and YAC (Youth Activities Club) to name a few of the various names given to the organizations which helped entertain the dependent children of U.S. servicemen. Most of the organizations survived through parent volunteers and received a large amount of their operating capital from fund-raisers such as postwide fairs. These events were open to the public (i.e., the Germans).

There would be military equipment displays, demonstrations, rides, games, and, more importantly to the Germans, the opportunity to partake of three American delicacies—Dentyne chewing gum, American-style ice cream, and most of all, grilled American hamburgers with all the trimmings. These three items would literally be sold by the truckloads. The Germans already had the market cornered in beer, bratwurst, pretzels, and wiener schnitzels.

J. Lamar and Peggy Sue Ann had had the distinct pleasure of selling chewing gum and making ice cream sundaes at previous fairs. J. Lamar literally had chocolate syrup dripping off his elbows after one such sundae session.

Getting to work in a hamburger booth provided one of the more humorous thought-provoking situations to J. Lamar and a buddy of his from Boston, Christopher Patrick Houlihan (you didn't get much more Irish than Christy Pat). It became the lot of J. Lamar and Christy Pat to be in charge of the condiments. (No, they weren't trying to promote safe sex—only dressing up the hamburgers.)

The condiments consisted of the normal items—ketchup, mustard, mayonnaise, pickles, and of course, onions. However, these were no ordinary onions. These were the dehydrated type which, if properly prepared, were soaked in copious amounts of water for approximately twenty minutes in order to be reconstituted. Well, as you might imagine, the requirements for onions became too much to keep up with. Try as they might, J. Lamar and Christy Pat could not keep enough reconstituted onions available. If you can visualize it, a no. 10 can or teaspoon of dehydrated onions when mixed with water or any liquid would expand about three times its dry state. (Keep this thought in your mind.)

After awhile, J. Lamar and Christy Pat began putting dry, dehydrated, unreconstituted onions out on the condiment line. The Germans, always looking for a good deal, piled on the dry onions (average of three spoons to each hamburger).

At this point it should be mentioned that located next to the hamburger stand was the German beer tent. Guess where the Germans with their dry onion laden hamburgers went to eat? You got it. After a few trips to the beer tent on their own, J. Lamar and Christy Pat began thinking and laughing about the gastrointestinal reactions that surely must have been caused when the dry onions and beer were mixed. They conjured up various scenarios of a couple named Herman and Helga as they went through the evening after consuming their dry onion hamburgers and beer.

This made the "tour of duty" as condiment controllers go by much faster. It also provided many laughs throughout the following weeks as J. Lamar and Christy Pat went on their noontime runs.

I Beg Your Pardon

As previously indicated, J. Lamar ran into and served with some real characters in the military. One such individual was Captain Vladamir Wasniewski—"Ski" to most people.

Ski possessed many traits which some people found amusing, some found interesting, and some found totally perplexing. The higher the rank, the more perplexing Ski could be. To say he could be considered unconventional would be an understatement. The one thing J. Lamar and others liked about Ski was that you never had to guess where he stood on an issue or situation. He was as subtle as a thumb in the eye.

Due to his rather rough background and overall character, Ski did not care for some of the pomp and ceremony of the Army traditions. One such tradition was the commanding officers' New Year's Day reception which gave J. Lamar an opportunity to witness Ski at his best.

These receptions usually took place in the afternoon or early evening on New Year's Day at the Officers' Club or at the commander's quarters ("home" to you civilians). The receptions also required the officers and their wives to dress in proper attire. For the officers this meant dress blues; for the women this meant cocktail dresses. Rather spiffy occasion.

During one such "command performance," J. Lamar and Peggy Sue Ann happened to be in the receiving line behind Ski. Ski, being a bachelor, basically tolerated married women. The single variety became another situation. As the receiving line moved forward so all could give their salutations to the commanding officer, J. Lamar detected that Ski may have been at the bar just a tad too long and that some of his remarks appeared to be getting to a major and his wife in front of him.

However, the action that provoked the young major to break his silence and forbearance was not what Ski said but what he did. Appearing to be trying to be unobtrusive, Ski passed gas which sounded like a machine gun on a firing range.

At that point, the major's head whipped around and he stated point blank to Ski, "I beg your pardon; do you realize you just broke wind in front of my wife?"

To which Ski replied "Hell, Sir, I'm sorry. I didn't realize it was her turn."

To say the least, J. Lamar had to admire the quick wit of Ski even though he thought his actions were a bit much. Of course, Peggy Sue Ann had been witness to the event and chided J. Lamar because he turned his back and laughed. The young major just turned his head. He knew he had met his match in Captain Vladimir Wasniewski.

Dumpster 1, J. Lamar 0

Having survived the tour of duty in Germany, J. Lamar and his family returned to the land of kudzu vine, coon dogs, and country music—Fort Bragg, North Carolina. Remember, the first time at this post, J. Lamar was a student at the Special Forces School. This time around, he would again be at the school but as an instructor/chief of the division which conducted the training for the young Special Forces officers-to-be.

This particular tour also put him in touch with an officer with whom he had served in Vietnam—General Jumping Joe Carl Lucas, commandant of the United States Army Institute of Military Assistance (USAIMA). The name Jumping Joe Carl did not mean he jumped up and down or around; it meant he liked to jump (parachute) from all types of aircraft. This fact and the relationship between J. Lamar and Jumping Joe Carl gave J. Lamar one of his more memorable jump stories.

As you may also remember, one of the facets of Special Forces training involved airborne operations. The students learned how to properly set up LZs (landing zones) and DZs (drop zones) in order to receive resupply of men and material. Sounds simple and it basically is. During one such training session, the aircraft to be used for the class was a Twin Otter (a small two-engine aircraft).

In a round-robin arrangement, teams of students would set up an LZ to land the Twin Otter. The Twin Otter had the capability known as STOL—short take off landing. Therefore, not much of a runway was required. A fairly level short open field would suffice. Once on the ground, other students, three to four at a time, would load on the Twin Otter and would parachute to a DZ also set up by other students. They all got a chance to participate in all three events—LZ, DZ, and a jump. You get the picture.

Enter J. Lamar and Jumping Joe Carl. J. Lamar called Jumping Joe and told him about the class and the Twin Otter. Jumping Joe was ready to go. They flew out to the training site by helicopter and actually became the first group to jump—J. Lamar, Jumping Joe, and his aide, a young lieutenant.

All proceeded as planned. The Twin Otter took off and made the approach to the DZ. To exit the Twin Otter, you basically had to sit on the floor, scoot to the door on your butt, and then push yourself out the door away from the aircraft using an equal push with each hand. Sounds simple, but it can get hairy.

Jumping Joe went first followed by J. Lamar and then the aide. Almost immediately, J. Lamar perceived two things had not gone according to plan. Jumping Joe had pushed too strong with one hand which made him turn while his chute deployed and left him with twisted suspension lines. Add to this heavy winds at jump altitude (approximately two thousand feet). While Jumping Joe worked at getting his suspension lines untwisted, the high winds carried him

away from the DZ toward the trees. He would not be able to control his chute until he got the lines untwisted.

J. Lamar had not twisted and was able to control his chute in order to hold against the wind. The aide knew where his bread was buttered and turned his chute to track with the wind and catch up with Jumping Joe although knowing this would put him landing off the DZ in the trees.

At this point, J. Lamar thought he had all under control. He did, except for one small set of details. As he observed his possible landing area, he detected a flat rectangular object with symmetrically placed "dots" around it. As the ground came closer, J. Lamar determined the object was a concrete slab from a building which apparently had been torn down. The "dots" were fence posts. He immediately turned his chute to track with the wind and hoped to pass over these obstacles. You must remember the ground is quickly approaching.

As he passed over the "hazards," J. Lamar turned his chute back to hold against wind in order to keep from going into the trees. He again observed his possible landing area, and much to his dismay, saw a green object which appeared to be a small low shed directly in his line to land. The concrete slab and fence posts had caught his attention and he had not seen the green object.

Once again he turned his chute to track with the wind but he ran out of air space. J. Lamar landed about three feet in front of the green object. He ducked his head, threw out his left arm and bounced off the green object.

The green object was a Dempsey dumpster. Why or how it was left there no one knew.

J. Lamar survived the landing with a fractured wrist, a sprained ankle, bruised body, and a hell of a jump story. How many people do you know who have parachuted into a dumpster?

By the way, General Jumping Joe and his aide did land in the trees but with no problems. Of course, Jumping Joe also had a good story to tell.

The students did not miss an opportunity to get J. Lamar. Displayed prominently on the classroom blackboard the next day was the score: Dumpster 1, J. Lamar 0.

Epilogue

As they say, all good things must come to an end. J. Lamar ended his journeys in the military after twenty-one years. He retired back to his native state of Tennessee—home of the Grand Ole Opry, Jack Daniel's Tennessee Sour Mash Whiskey, and Big Orange football. He thought he had died and gone to heaven.

What became readily apparent is that things had changed and the surroundings he left at an earlier age were not the same. Maybe it's because he had changed from the vast experiences of being in the army. J. Lamar realized he had had the privilege and honor to serve with America's finest—her soldiers. "The GI."

Acronyms

AAR	After Action Report
ADC	Assistant Division Commander
ADP	Automated Data Processing
ADPRID	Advance Degree Program for Instructor Duty
AER	Army Emergency Relief
AG	Adjutant General
AO	Area of Operation
APC	Armored Personnel Carrier
ASAP	As Soon as Possible
AWOL	Absent without Leave
BEO	Brigade Executive Officer
BG	Brigadier General
BIC	Briefer in Charge
BUFE	Big Ugly Frigging Elephant
CGSC	Command and General Staff College
CINC	Commander in Chief
COMUSMACV	Commander, United States Military Assistance Command, Vietnam
CONEX	Container, Exchange
CONUS	Continental United States
CP	Command Post
C-RATIONS	Combat Rations
CRS	Couldn't Remember Sh—
DA	Department of the Army
DAC	Dependent Activities Council
DISCOM	Division Support Command

DYA	Dependent Youth Activities
DYC	Dependent Youth Council
DZ	Drop Zone
EDRE	Emergency Deployment Readiness Exercise
ETO	European Theater of Operations
FTX	Field Training Exercise
FUBAR	Fouled Up Beyond All Recognition
FUBB	Fouled Up Beyond Belief
GI	Government Issue
GOBS	Good Ol' Boy Soldier
IIC	Inspector in Charge
IOAC	Infantry Officer Advance Course
JAG	Judge Advocate General
KP	Kitchen Police
LTC (RET)	Lieutenant Colonel (Retired)
LZ	Landing Zone
MP	Military Police
MRE	Meals Ready to Eat
NATO	North Atlantic Treaty Organization
NCO	Noncommissioned Officer
NCOIC	Noncommissioned Officer in Charge
NORTHAG	Northern Army Group
OG	Officer of the Guard
OIC	Officer in Charge
PFC	Private First Class
PLF	Parachute Landing Fall
POM	Post-Operation Maintenance
POM	Preparation for Overseas Movement
POMCUS	Propositioned Material Configures to Unit Sets
PT	Physical Training
R & R	Rest & Relaxation
REFORGER	Return of Forces to Germany
REMF	Rear Echelon M—— F——
RHIP	Rank Has Its Privilege
SEC	Southeastern Conference

SFC	Sergeant First Class
STOL	Short Take Off—Landing
TO & E	Table of Organization & Equipment
UCMJ	Uniform Code of Military Justice
USAIMA	United States Army Institute for Military Assistance
USAREUR	United States Army, Europe
USO	United Services Organization
XO	Executive Officer
YAC	Youth Activities Council